Logibeasts
A User's Guide

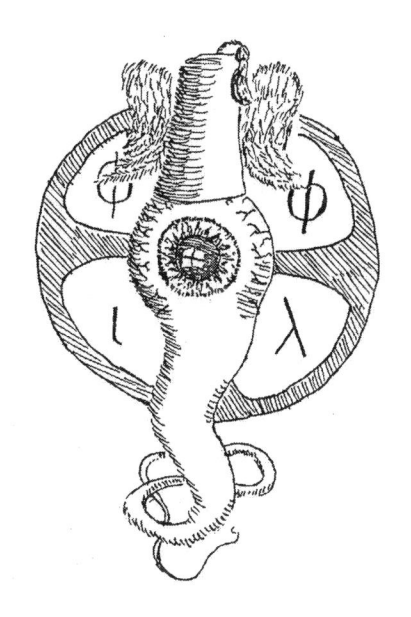

Josh Dever

Artwork by
Maeve Dever

Copyright © 2018 Josh Dever
Illustrations copyright © 2018 Maeve Dever

All rights reserved

First printing, August 2018

CONTENTS

1 Logibeast Genealogies and the Logibestiary   **7**
    1.1   Logibeasts and Their Families   9
    1.2   A Brief Tour of Mutant Logibeasts   18

2 Logibeast Genetic Engineering   **27**
    2.1   A Brief Introduction to Logibeast Genetic Recipes .   28
    2.2   Grotesque Merge and Split   30
    2.3   Primeval Merge and Split   33
    2.4   Winged Merge and Split   37
    2.5   Bloodthirsty Merge and Split   42
    2.6   Eldritch Merge and Split   46
    2.7   Brief Review of the Genetic Methods   49
    2.8   Some Sample Recipes   52

3 Elemental Attacks and Elemental Vulnerabilities   **55**
    3.1   The Bloodthirsty Rule   59
    3.2   The Grotesque Rule   71
    3.3   The Eldritch Rule   78
    3.4   The Primeval Rule   86
    3.5   The Winged Rule   92
    3.6   Logibeast Vulnerabilities   98
    3.7   Brief Review of Logibeast Elemental Theory   102

4 Dueling With Logibeasts   **105**
    4.1   Alpha and Omega   114
    4.2   The Three True Outcomes   123

4.3	A Step-By-Step Guide to Logibeast Dueling	128
4.4	Designer Dueling	135

5 Grand Unified Logibeast Theory — 155
5.1	Proof of the First Result	156
5.2	Proof of the Second Result	160
5.3	A Brief Glance at Grand Unified Logibeast Theory	165

6 The Logibestiary — 169

WELCOME!

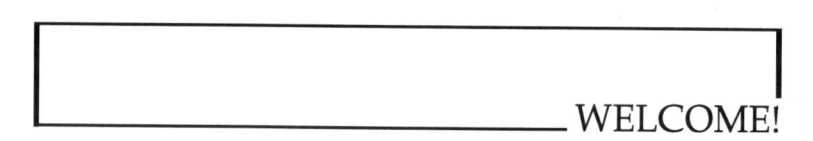

... to the wonderful and frightening world of Logibeasts! Whether you are a xenocollector interested in building up your own private zoo of exotic and unusual Logibeasts, or a budding genetic engineer eager to explore what odd new permutations you can extract from the Logibeast genome, or a would-be duelist out to build deadly Logibeasts and put them to trial by combat in the arena, or even a theoretician-in-the-making more interested in *understanding* the world of Logibeasts than dirtying your hands with the actual doing, we've got you covered. Your brand-new, state-of-the-art Logibeast™ Home Genetic Laboratory (HGL) provides everything you need to explore all of these paths through Logibeast territory. Read through this easy guidebook, and within hours you can be using your Logibeast HGL to produce everything from the humble Aarobak to the exotic Eldritch Zyrrhaur.

You should first familiarize yourself with the contents of your HGL kit. The kit contains:

- A collection of Logibeast eggs, each labelled with the kind of beast it will produce.

- The Logibestiary, your definitive catalog of Logibeasts and their ancestries.

- The actual Genetic Manipulator, capable of performing such operations as the Bloodthirsty Merge and the Primeval Split.

- Your very own Genetic Logbook, in which you can record genetic recipes for producing all of your favorite beasts.

- The Logizoo 2.0 storage facility, guaranteed to contain safely up to a dozen Logibeasts of any variety.

- A Beginner's Arena, suitable for getting started with Logibeast combat. (The Beginner's Arena warranty covers only the first three combats. For the more serious duelist, we recommend investing in the TuffArena, which can be expected to survive at least a dozen combats with only minimal wear and tear.)

Once you've familiarized yourself with these components, start working through the guidebook. We'll take you through five major stages. First, we'll fill in a little history of the Logibeasts and learn how to create helpful beast genealogies. Second, we'll learn how to use the Genetic Manipulator and master all the genetic engineering methods needed to produce beasts of your own. Third, we'll introduce you to the peculiar world of Logibeast elemental theory so that you'll know what kinds of dangers to expect from the creatures you've engineered. Fourth, we'll put those dangers to work, mastering the rules and techniques of Logibeast dueling. Fifth (as a bit of a break from the blood and violence) we'll give a very short introduction to high Logibeast theory, sketching the outlines of the recently established Grand Unified Theory of Logibeasts. And now, to work!

CHAPTER 1
LOGIBEAST GENEALOGIES AND THE LOGIBESTIARY

You know the basic story, of course. About a billion years ago, during the height of the Rodinian supercontinent, the São Francisco-Congo craton fractured into the separate São Francisco and Congo cratons. In their wake was left the Walvian subcraton. The Walvian subcraton, for reasons still quite poorly understood, was then home to an extraordinary period of biological flourishing and diversity. While most of the world saw nothing more sophisticated than clumps of blue-green algae, the Walvian subcraton was swarming with... well, with just about everything you can imagine, and probably quite a few things that you can't, or wish you couldn't.

While there is no compelling evidence that what have come to be known as *Logibeasts* had anything like human intelligence (in particular, the Silurian hypothesis, while not decisively refutable on the basis of the scientifically credible evidence, has never achieved more than a fringe following), there is no doubt that these creatures extensively explored evolutionary pathways that the rest of life on earth has never ventured down. For almost a hundred million years, Primeval J'jaklus swarmed over the Walvian plateaus and Eldritch Foorghasts made their strange ways through dark passages of the Walvian mountains. But then the Tonian LLSVP Subduction Crisis sent the Walvian subcraton to the bottom of the

Braziliano Ocean, and the reign of the Logibeasts came to a sudden end.

There things remained, with the Logbeasts forgotten by history, until the 1993 Cavendish expedition, exploring the Atlantic seafloor near Tristan da Cunha, found unexpected fossilized remains in ground samples they had extracted. Much to their surprise, the Cavendish team discovered that there were viable DNA strands in many of these fossils. Even more to their surprise, the DNA turned out to diverge quite radically from all known species. Once a team of Vietnamese geneticists worked out that the recovered DNA included pyrimidine and and purine base pairs to create a *six-letter* genetic code, mapping of the Logibeast genome proceeded rapidly.

It was then that a genetic engineering scheme of a scale and vision that put Jurassic Park (and all of its many sequels) to shame was (if you'll pardon the pun) hatched. Early efforts at implanting Logibeast DNA strands in sheep embryos proved that Logibeast genes are extraordinarily friendly to cloning and manipulation, and within a few years Latvian teams had succeeded in producing actual Aarobaks and Oolopods in the laboratory. For a while Logibeast engineering was confined first to several genetic research institutes around the world, and then to a sanctuary region inside the Chernobyl Exclusion Zone. But it didn't take long for the forces of capitalism to triumph – as public fascination with the diversity of Logibeasts grew, a number of biotech startups began selling kits for home production of Logibeasts.

After the Santa Fe incident of 2006, it was recognized that greater oversight of Logibeast engineering was needed, and under a UN mandate Logitech^{TM} was established as the only licensed provider of home genetic engineering facilities for Logibeasts. And so here you are, proud owner of a Logitech HGL and a welcome new member of the Logibeast family.

We know you're eager to leap in and start building your very own Logibeasts. But bear with us a bit longer. Before you can get started with your Genetic Manipulator, you need to know a bit about Logibeast breeding. That's a bit ironic, because modern-day Logibeasts won't breed at all. The only way we get more of them is through our various genetic experimentations. But it turns out that, although it's now been some nine hundred million years since there was a real Logibeast birth, it's still crucial to understanding their genetic structure to know a lot about their genealogy. *You won't get anywhere building a Logibeast in the lab if you don't know everything about how a beast of that sort once was born in the wild.*

1.1 Logibeasts and Their Families

There are a *lot* of different Logibeasts. Current genetic engineering methods have already produced 50 species, and that number is growing all the time. (With the aid of your HGL, you might be the next one to construct a Logibeast that humanity has never seen before.) But that number pales in comparison to the variety of Logibeasts once wandering the wilds of the Walvian subcraton. Fossil evidence is still inconclusive on exactly how diverse the Logibeast population was, we can tell from examination of he Logibeast genome that an enormous number of species *could* have sprung from the core genetic material. Experts are split between the conservative camp holding that there are 4,294,967,296 possible Logibeast varieties and the liberal camp holding that there are infinitely many possible varieties. In any case, it's a big number.

Fortunately, despite that bewildering variety, there is a bit of phylogenetic structure to the Logibeast world. At the heart of the Logibeast world are the so-called *basic* Logibeasts. There are five of these: the Aarobak, the Fluftoom, the Oolopod, the Schloof, and the Yttrig. In addition to the five basic Logibeasts there are five great phyla of beasts, each of which contains a potentially enormous number of different species. There are the *Grotesque* Logibeasts, such as the Grotesque Ogrit and the Grotesque Uuhulmo. There are the *Primeval* Logibeasts, such as the Primeval Schniftoo and the Primeval Knug. There are the *Winged* Logibeasts, such as the Winged Hvornid and the Winged Shugraat. There are the *Bloodthirsty* Logibeasts, such as the Bloodthirsty Chylziq and the Bloodthirsty Cavaidko. And finally there are the *Eldritch* Logibeasts, such as the Eldritch Whylxot. Every beast that isn't one of the basic five is either Grotesque, Primeval, Winged, Bloodthirsty, or Eldritch.

Again, contemporary Logibeasts won't breed, which is why we (and now you) are forced to use genetic manipulation to create the beasts we want. But in the wild, Logibeasts had mothers and fathers just like we do. (Well, usually, and kind of like we do. Some complexities will emerge.) And to be a successful Logibeast builder, you need to understand the natural hereditary patterns of Logibeasts.

All Logibeasts hatch from eggs. For most Logibeasts, those eggs came (in the wild) from the beast's parents. But not the basic Logibeasts. Basic Logibeasts don't have parents. Don't ask where their eggs come from. Three leading Logibeast scientists in 2009 led an expedition into a large Logibeast fossil deposit to try to find the source of the eggs – one never returned and the other two spent the remainder of their days in an asylum. That pretty much shut down research into that topic.) So when it comes to ancestry, there's not much to say about the basic Logibeasts.

For the other beasts, though, there is a helpful story to tell. Grotesque, Primeval, Winged, and Bloodthirsty beasts all have both mother and father. Any two Logibeasts can have offspring of all four of those types. An Oolopd and a Fluftoom, for example, can give birth to:

- A Grotesque Gnuffle
- A Primeval Dessifto
- A Winged Xeerun
- A Bloodthirsty Awtroof

(Our current understanding is that various subtle Logirituals performed during the Logimating determine the type of offspring produced, but to date no one has had the intestinal fortitude to investigate carefully.)

Again, because they won't breed in captivity, you aren't going to get yourself a Grotesque Gnuffle by getting an Oolopod and a Fluftoom to have little baby Gnuffles. But in order to genetically manipulate your way into a Grotesque Gnuffle, you'll need to know that Grotesque Gnuffles in the wild are offspring of Oolopods and Fluftooms.

That is, you need to be able to make a *family tree* for the Grotesque Gnuffle. It's not much of a tree, but here it is:

1.1. LOGIBEASTS AND THEIR FAMILIES

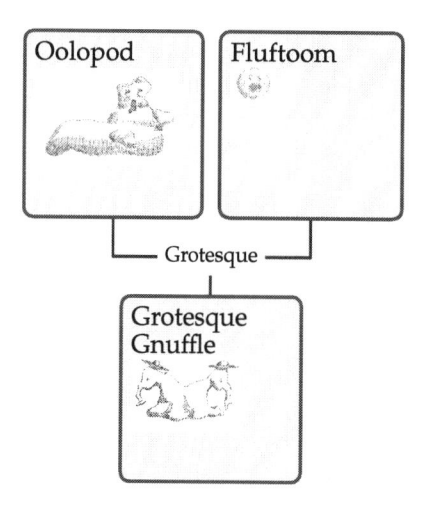

Let's go through the various bits of information encoded in this tree. We have the three Logibeasts involved – the Oolopod and Fluftoom parents, and the Grotesque Gnuffle offspring. And we have charming pictures of all three, so that we can start getting used to the appearances of these strange creatures. We have a tree structure representing the Oolopod and the Fluftoom as the parents, and the branching of the tree is marked as "Grotesque" to remind us that the Grotesque Gnuffle is the result when the Oolopod and the Fluftoom reproduce in the specifically Grotesque manner.

But what if you didn't happen already to know that the Grotesque Gnuffle was the Grotesque offspring of an Oolopod and a Fluftoom? Or didn't know what these beasts looked like? How then would you learn what you needed to know to put together a family tree for the Gnuffle?

We've got you covered. We have provided you with an up-to-date information-rich *Logibestiary* (found at the end of this handy guide) containing all known genealogical information about Logibeasts. For example, open up your Logibestiary and turn to the *Grotesque Logibeast* section. There you will find this entry:

- Oolopod + Fluftoom $\Rightarrow$ Grotesque Gnuffle

This entry tells you the parents (on the left side of the arrow, with mother listed first and father listed second) and the offspring (on the right side of the arrow). And you'll find a likeness of the

Grotesque Gnuffle there as well. (To see what the Oolopod and Fluftoom look like, then turn to the *Basic Logibeasts* section of the Logibestiary.)

Let's now talk a bit more about mothers and fathers. Grotesque, Winged, and Bloodthirsty beasts are indifferent to the difference between mother and father. If a mother Oolopod and a father Fluftoom have a Grotesque baby, it will be a Grotesque Gnuffle. And if a mother Fluftoom and a father Oolopod have a Grotesque baby, it will also be a Grotesque Gnuffle. But for Primeval beasts, the roles of mother and father matter. When a mother Oolopod and a father Aarobak have a Primeval baby, it's a Primeval J'jaklu. But when a mother Aarobak and a father Oolopod have a Primeval baby, it's a Primeval Gtuftbak. So consider two family trees:

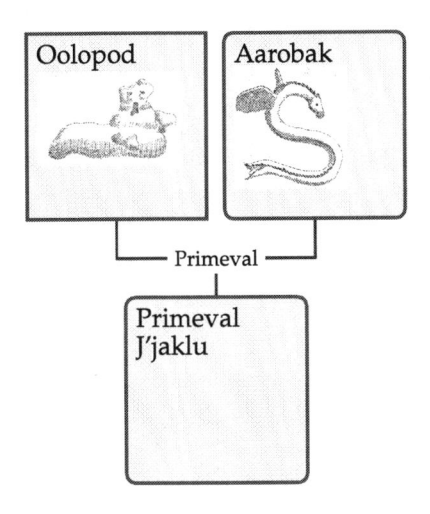

```
┌─────────┐ ┌─────────┐
│ Oolopod │ │ Aarobak │
│         │ │         │
│         │ │         │
└────┬────┘ └────┬────┘
     └─ Primeval ─┘
          │
     ┌─────────┐
     │ Primeval│
     │ J'jaklu │
     │         │
     └─────────┘
```

and:

1.1. LOGIBEASTS AND THEIR FAMILIES

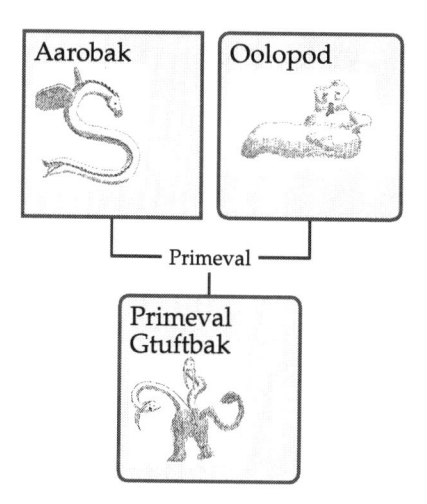

Notice that the Oolopod mother of the Primeval J'jaklu and the Aarobak mother of the Primeval Gtuftbak are in boxes with squared, rather than rounded, corners. That lets us, for Primeval beasts, distinguish mother and father. Any given Logibeast could be either mother or father – in fact, the very same beast could be mother to one offspring and father to another. (We're still not entirely sure what *mother* and *father* meant for Logibeasts. The eggs were not laid by the mother, but by the two parents collectively. Work by metaphysicians of sex and gender has been exploring this question extensively in recent years, with little progress to date.)

Because it *sometimes* matters, the Logibestiary keeps track of the mother/father distinction. (First mother then father, in each entry.) But for Grotesque, Winged, and Bloodthirsty beasts, the mother/father roles can be reversed, and we won't mark the mother/father distinction on their family trees.

That leaves the Eldritch beasts. Eldritch beasts are the result of a peculiar (and, frankly, rather disturbing) parthenogenesis process that all Logibeasts can undergo. As a result, Eldritch beasts have only one parent, not two. That's reflected in their Logibestiary entries, such as:

- Aarobak ⇒ Eldritch Webblob

- Eldritch Webblob ⇒ Eldritch Mumfloom

So an Aarobak can "give birth to", via parthenogenesis, an Eldritch Webblob. And that Eldritch Webblob can, in turn, give parthenogenetic birth to an Eldritch Mumfloom. That lets us put together a family tree for the Eldritch Mumfloom:

Aarobak

|
Eldritch
|
Eldritch Webblob

|
Eldritch
|
Eldritch Mumfloom

That's all as it was inn the wild, of course. If you want an Eldritch beast, you're going to need to build it in the lab.

The Eldritch Mumfloom is a *second generation* Logibeast. That's because there are *two* generations above it in its family tree. Its parent the Eldritch Webblob is a *first generation* Logibeast, and its grandparent the Aarobak is a *zeroeth generation*, or *original* Logibeast.

The Eldritch Mumfloom is hardly the only second-generation Logibeast. Consider the Bloodthirsty Chylziq. Consulting your Logibestiary, you'll learn that a Bloodthirsty Chylziq has a Fluftoom and an Eldritch Foorghast as parents. The Eldritch Foorghast then has a Fluftoom as its parent. (Maybe even the same Fluftoom!) Now we can make a family tree:

1.1. LOGIBEASTS AND THEIR FAMILIES

```
        ┌──────────┐
        │ Fluftoom │
        └────┬─────┘
             │ Eldritch
┌──────────┐ ┌──────────┐
│ Fluftoom │ │ Eldritch │
│          │ │ Foorghast│
└────┬─────┘ └────┬─────┘
     └─ Bloodthirsty ─┘
              │
      ┌───────────────┐
      │  Bloodthirsty │
      │    Chylziq    │
      └───────────────┘
```

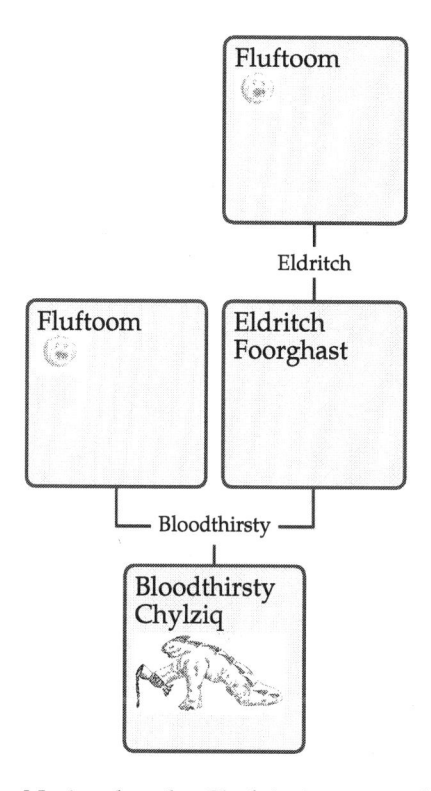

Notice that the Chylziq is a second-generation beast because the *longest* chain of ancestry for the Chylziq goes back two steps.

There are also third generation Logibeasts, such as the Primeval Vrikvriktu. Again consulting the Logibestiary, we learn:

1. A Primeval Vrilvriktu has a Grotesque Ffli as mother and an Eldritch Iumhfiss as father.

2. A Grotesque Ffli has a Yttrig and an Eldritch Webblob as parents.

3. An Eldritch Webblob has an Aarobak as parent.

4. An Eldritch Iumhfiss has an Oolopod as parent.

Putting together the pieces, we get this family tree:

CHAPTER 1. LOGIBEAST GENEALOGIES

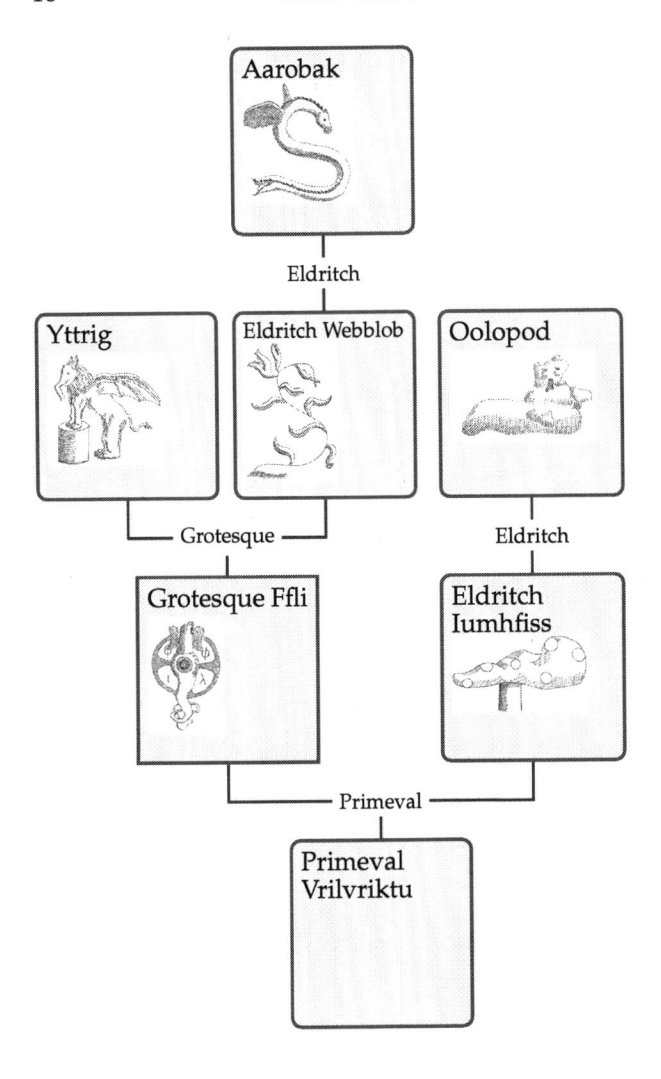

```
                    ┌──────────┐
                    │ Aarobak  │
                    └────┬─────┘
                       Eldritch
      ┌──────────┬──────┴──────┬──────────┐
  ┌───┴───┐  ┌───────────────┐  ┌──────────┐
  │Yttrig │  │Eldritch Webblob│  │ Oolopod │
  └───┬───┘  └───────┬───────┘  └────┬─────┘
      └──Grotesque───┘            Eldritch
              │                       │
      ┌───────┴───────┐       ┌───────┴──────┐
      │ Grotesque Ffli│       │   Eldritch   │
      │               │       │   Iumhfiss   │
      └───────┬───────┘       └───────┬──────┘
              └──────── Primeval ─────┘
                        │
                ┌───────┴───────┐
                │   Primeval    │
                │  Vrilvriktu   │
                └───────────────┘
```

As of the current edition of the Logibestiary, the beasts of the highest generational count are the Grotesque Uuhulmo and the Grotesque Hjunkit, both of which are *sixth* generation Logibeasts. Here, for example, is the family tree for the Grotesque Uuhulmo:

1.1. LOGIBEASTS AND THEIR FAMILIES

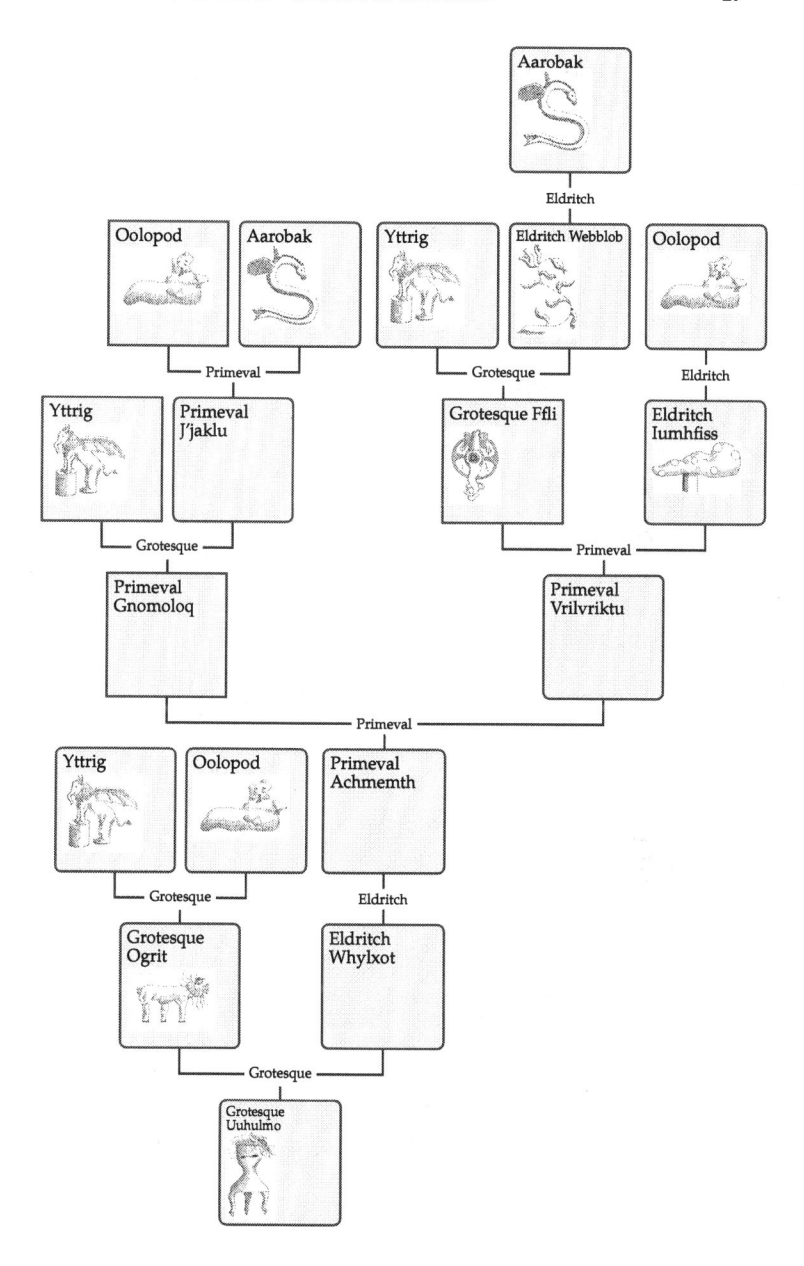

That's quite something!

You're going to spend a lot of time writing out family trees for

Logibeasts, first to help you plan genetic engineering of the creatures you want, and then even more later to help you plan combat between Logibeasts. So get used to flipping around in that Logibestiary. With time, though, you'll get familiar with a lot of the common Logibeast varieties and be able to write up their genealogy in your sleep.

1.2 A Brief Tour of Mutant Logibeasts

You'll already have noticed that there isn't much to Logibeast family trees – it's a rather simple skill to master. Nevertheless, there are some surprising genetic regularities of the Logibeasts hidden away in this basic genealogy. To bring out these regularities, let's take a brief look at some known mutations of the Logibeast world. These are all creatures whose former existence we can detect in the fossil record, but whose genetic structure differed too greatly from the mainline Logibeast genome for us to be able to recreate with genetic engineering.

1. All existing Logibeasts have zero parents (the basic Logibeasts), one parent (the Eldritch Logibeasts) or two parents (the Grotesque, Primeval, Bloodthirsty, and Winged Logibeasts). But at one point there was a small sixth phylum of Logibeasts whose members had *three* parents. These were the Howling Logibeasts. The Howling Opfringo, for example, was the offspring of an Aarobak, an Oolopod, and a Yttrig:

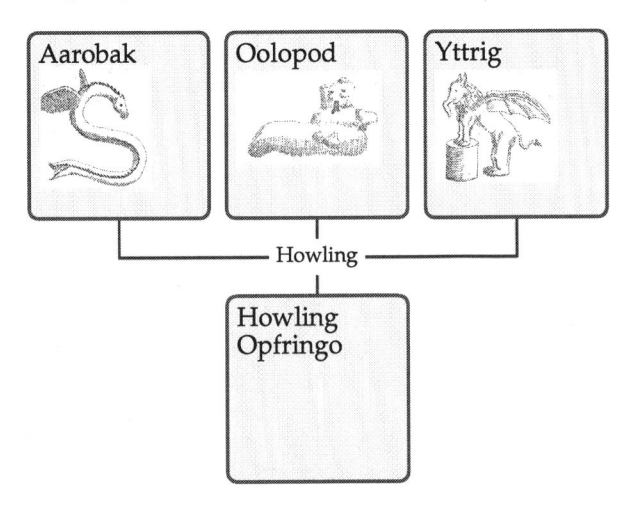

1.2. A BRIEF TOUR OF MUTANT LOGIBEASTS

(We're afraid that the fragmentary genetic material isn't enough for us to venture even an artist's reproduction of the appearance of the Howling Opfringo.) The evidence suggests that the Howling creatures, like the Primeval creatures, had distinct parental roles, so that the Howling Opfringo, for example, had the Aarobak specifically as its mother, the Oolopod specifically as its father, and the Yttrig specifically as its ... well, the current leading candidate label is *semi-uncle*.

For better or worse, you aren't going to be able to make Howling creatures – these strange mutants are well outside the range of current technology. Every creature you'll need to deal with has at most two parents.

2. At one point among the Eldritch creatures was the now-lost mutant *Eldritch Rhooit*. The curious thing about the Eldritch Rhooit is that its Eldritch parent was once again an Eldritch Rhooit. (Not the very same Rhooit. These were odd creatures, but not *that* odd.) An ordinary enough genealogical feature for a cow or a person, but not all what we normally find among the Logibeasts. So the family tree for an Eldritch Rhooit looks something like this:

```
┌─────────┐
│ Eldritch│
│ Rhooit  │
└────┬────┘
     │ Eldritch
┌────┴────┐
│ Eldritch│
│ Rhooit  │
└────┬────┘
     │ Eldritch
┌────┴────┐
│ Eldritch│
│ Rhooit  │
└────┬────┘
     │ Eldritch
┌────┴────┐
│ Eldritch│
│ Rhooit  │
└─────────┘
```

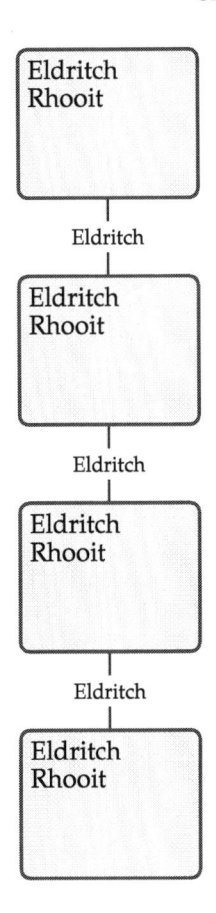

"Something like this" because that's actually only a fragment of the tree. Since the Eldritch Rhooit is its own Eldritch parent, the family tree goes back forever, with each Eldritch Rhooit in the tree introducing another Eldritch Rhooit as its parent. The Eldritch Rhooit is an example of what the experts call an *ungrounded* Logibeast, since its genetic tree never reaches its roots and thus never embeds in the ground.

The Eldritch Rhooit is not the only ungrounded mutant Logibeast we've found traces of. There are also the Eldritch Sfaurom and the Eldritch Gneesk. These two odd beasts have *each other* as Eldritch parents:

1.2. A BRIEF TOUR OF MUTANT LOGIBEASTS 21

```
┌─────────────┐
│ Eldritch    │
│ Gneesk      │
│             │
└──────┬──────┘
       │ Eldritch
┌──────┴──────┐
│ Eldritch Sfau- │
│ rom         │
│             │
└──────┬──────┘
       │ Eldritch
┌──────┴──────┐
│ Eldritch    │
│ Gneesk      │
│             │
└──────┬──────┘
       │ Eldritch
┌──────┴──────┐
│ Eldritch Sfau- │
│ rom         │
│             │
└─────────────┘
```

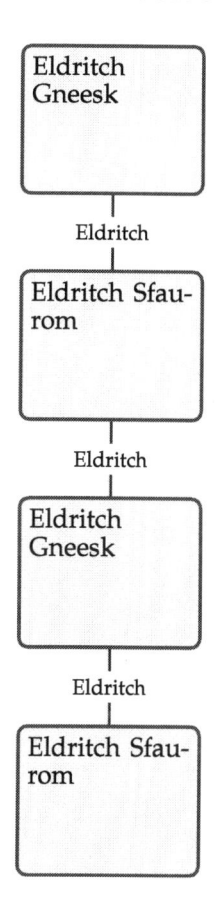

Once again both are ungrounded. The family tree goes back forever, alternating Sfaurom and Gneesk each generation.

Or there's the Winged X'dinkit. The Winged X'dinkit's parents are a Fluftoom and ... another Winged X'dinkit. So its family tree looks like this:

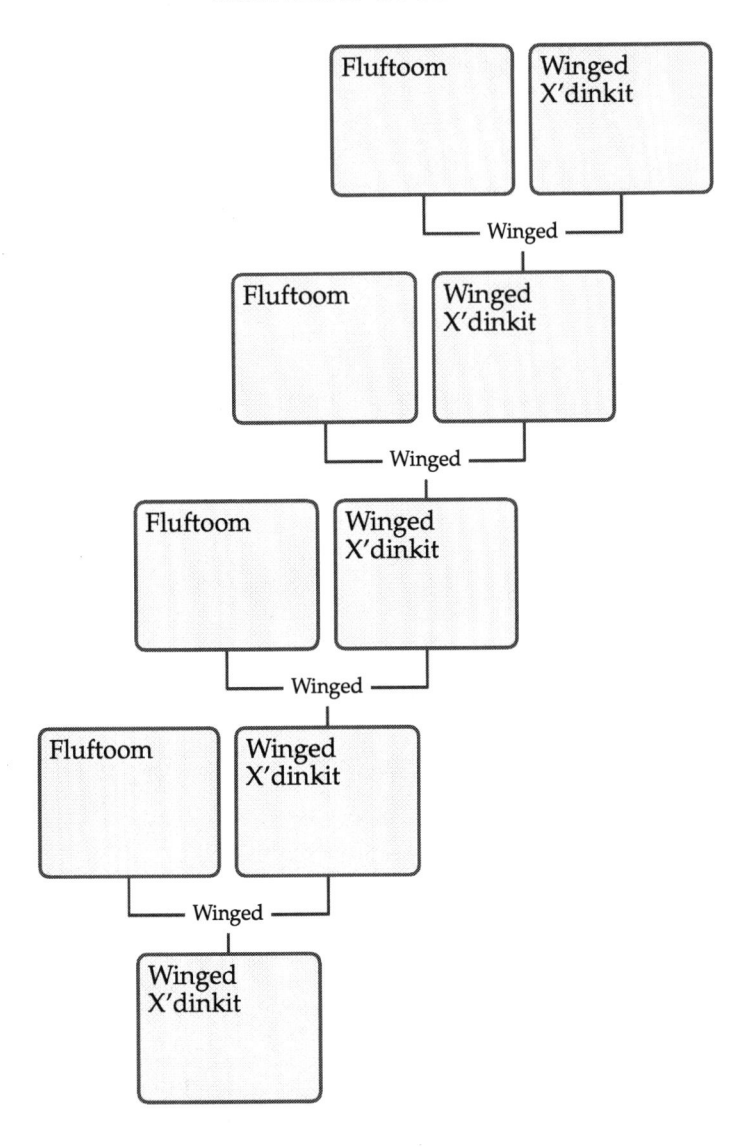

```
                    ┌──────────┐  ┌──────────┐
                    │ Fluftoom │  │ Winged   │
                    │          │  │ X'dinkit │
                    └────┬─────┘  └────┬─────┘
                         └─── Winged ──┘
                                │
              ┌──────────┐  ┌──────────┐
              │ Fluftoom │  │ Winged   │
              │          │  │ X'dinkit │
              └────┬─────┘  └────┬─────┘
                   └─── Winged ──┘
                          │
        ┌──────────┐  ┌──────────┐
        │ Fluftoom │  │ Winged   │
        │          │  │ X'dinkit │
        └────┬─────┘  └────┬─────┘
             └─── Winged ──┘
                    │
  ┌──────────┐  ┌──────────┐
  │ Fluftoom │  │ Winged   │
  │          │  │ X'dinkit │
  └────┬─────┘  └────┬─────┘
       └─── Winged ──┘
              │
        ┌──────────┐
        │ Winged   │
        │ X'dinkit │
        └──────────┘
```

The Fluftoom side of the Winged X'dinkit ancestry keeps coming to an end each generation, but each generation also reveals another level of Winged X'dinkit ancestry. Its family tree also goes back forever, and it's another ungrounded creature.

Fortunately, all of the Logibeasts that can be constructed

1.2. A BRIEF TOUR OF MUTANT LOGIBEASTS 23

with current technology are grounded creatures whose family trees come to an end, usually in just a few generations, so you don't need to worry about running out of room trying to write up the family tree of some creature you're trying to concoct.

3. One more odd mutant, and now lost, Logibeast. Consider the Bloodthirsty Frifroot. An Eldritch Rhooit and a Primeval Knug can have a Bloodthirsty Frifroot child, giving it this family tree:

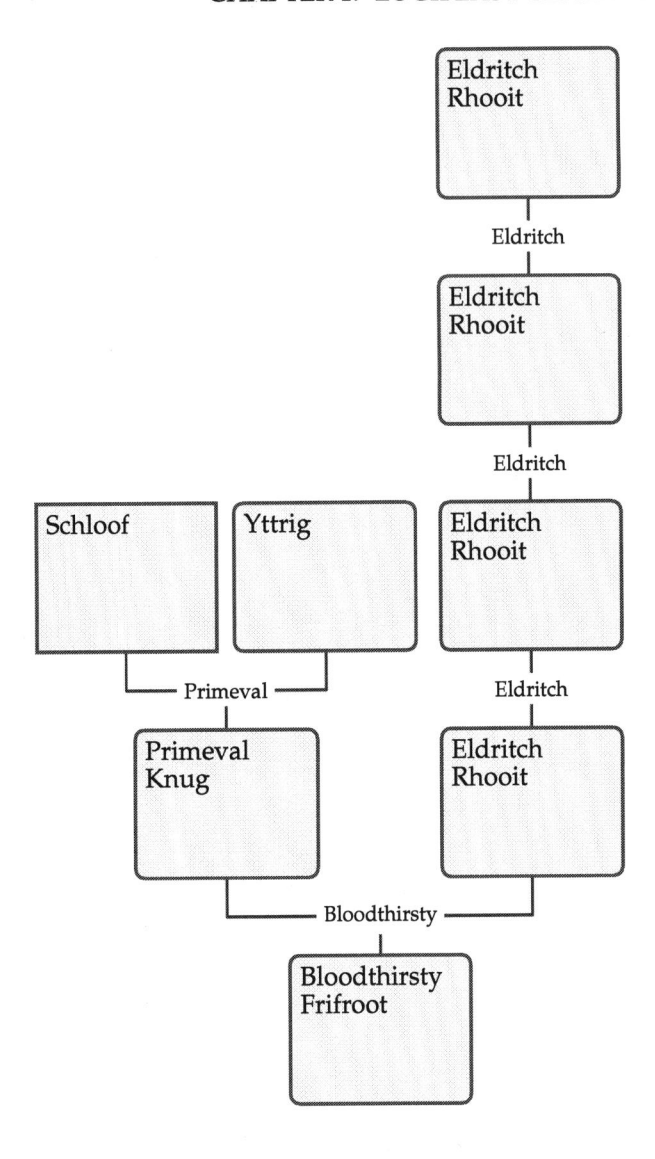

```
                    ┌─────────┐
                    │ Eldritch│
                    │ Rhooit  │
                    └────┬────┘
                       Eldritch
                    ┌────┴────┐
                    │ Eldritch│
                    │ Rhooit  │
                    └────┬────┘
                       Eldritch
┌────────┐ ┌────────┐ ┌────┴────┐
│ Schloof│ │ Yttrig │ │ Eldritch│
│        │ │        │ │ Rhooit  │
└───┬────┘ └────┬───┘ └────┬────┘
    └─ Primeval ─┘        Eldritch
       ┌────┴────┐    ┌────┴────┐
       │ Primeval│    │ Eldritch│
       │ Knug    │    │ Rhooit  │
       └────┬────┘    └────┬────┘
            └── Bloodthirsty ──┘
                     │
              ┌──────┴──────┐
              │ Bloodthirsty│
              │ Frifroot    │
              └─────────────┘
```

However, a Grotesque Gnuffle and an Eldritch Gneesk can *also* have a Bloodthirsty Frifroot child, which means it can also have this family tree:

1.2. A BRIEF TOUR OF MUTANT LOGIBEASTS 25

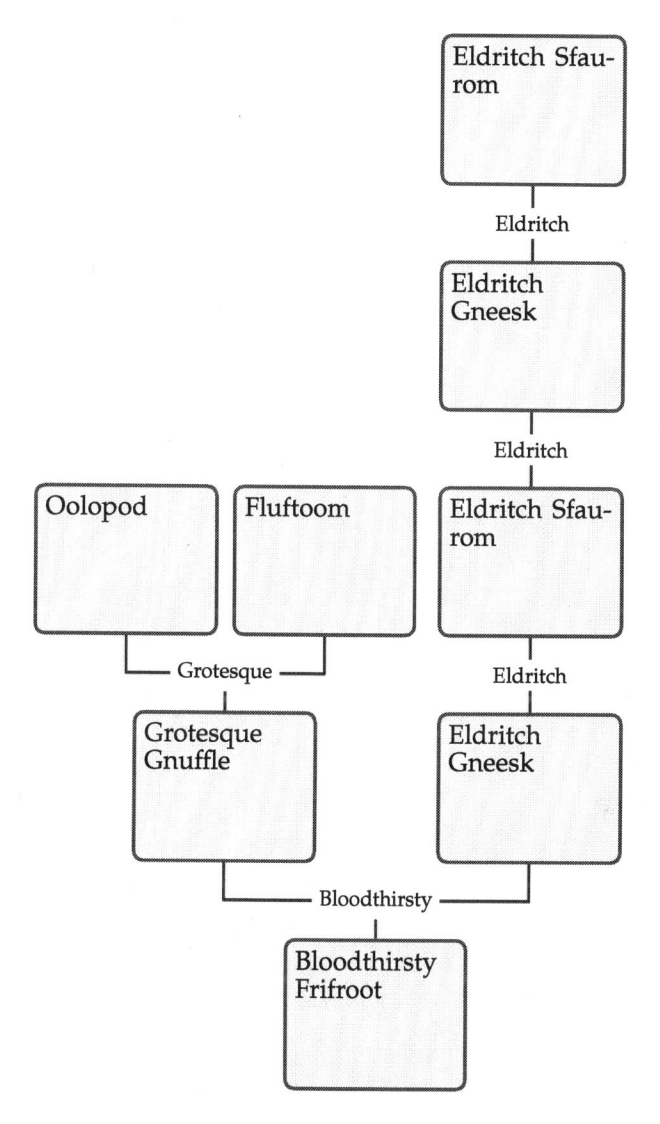

```
                          ┌──────────────┐
                          │ Eldritch Sfau-│
                          │ rom          │
                          └──────┬───────┘
                                 │ Eldritch
                          ┌──────┴───────┐
                          │ Eldritch     │
                          │ Gneesk       │
                          └──────┬───────┘
                                 │ Eldritch
  ┌──────────┐  ┌──────────┐  ┌──┴───────────┐
  │ Oolopod  │  │ Fluftoom │  │ Eldritch Sfau-│
  │          │  │          │  │ rom           │
  └────┬─────┘  └────┬─────┘  └──────┬───────┘
       └─ Grotesque ─┘               │ Eldritch
                │                 ┌──┴────────┐
       ┌────────┴──────┐          │ Eldritch  │
       │ Grotesque     │          │ Gneesk    │
       │ Gnuffle       │          └─────┬─────┘
       └────────┬──────┘                │
                └────── Bloodthirsty ───┘
                            │
                   ┌────────┴────────┐
                   │ Bloodthirsty    │
                   │ Frifroot        │
                   └─────────────────┘
```

Bloodthirsty Frifroots, then, can have two different family trees. They are, as we say in the business, of *dubious ancestry*. All of the existing Logibeasts, however, are of *indubious ancestry*. Each of them has a unique family tree, setting out the only possible collection of ancestors for that beast.

That's enough of a journey through the strange(r) world of mutant Logibeasts for now. We've seen enough to bring home the fact that the Logibeasts we *do* need to deal with have the nice features (features we might never even have noticed without seeing their absence among the mutants) of being grounded, of indubious ancestry, and of having at most two parents each.

CHAPTER 2
LOGIBEAST GENETIC ENGINEERING

Enough of all this history! Time to create some beasts. Unpack that Genetic Manipulator, plug it in (be sure to use a grounded outlet), and let's get going.

The first step is to talk about eggs. Eggs are *the* crucial ingredient in Logibeast genetic engineering. They are the source of the genetic material from which you will create the beasts of your wildest imagination. No eggs, no beasts. (Actually, that's not quite true. We'll see later how you can create some beasts that are, in a certain sense, egg-free. Vegan Logibeasts, we might call them. That's a bit of industry humor.) But eggs are more than just a source of genetic raw material. They are also crucial for the survival of Logibeasts.

A crucial thing to remember about all Logibeasts is that *even after they hatch*, they require the continued existence of their eggs to survive. If you destroy the egg of your adorable newborn Yttrig after it hatches, it will wither and die in a matter of minutes. (And trust us, you don't want a withered Yttrig on your hands.) The Genetic Manipulator contains a convenient Egg Storage Receptacle – we highly recommend keeping the eggs for any Loigbeasts you create in the ESR.

The typical Logibeast genetic engineering venture, then, goes like this in a nutshell (eggshell?): put one or more eggs in the ESR. Turn various dials and push various buttons for a while. (There's a bit of a theory to the turning and pushing. We'll be coming to that soon.) Eventually, out pops the Logibeast of your dreams. Keep the eggs for the beast in the ESR so that the empathic resonance between Logibeast and eggs is preserved and protected and the creature survives unharmed, and you've finished your experiment.

Now let's fill in a few missing details.

2.1 A Brief Introduction to Logibeast Genetic Recipes

We will soon move on to the exciting field of advanced Logibeast genetic manipulation, but first let's learn how to perform the basic operation of hatching an existing egg:

1. First, take an egg of your choice from your supply, and place it in the egg storage receptacle.

2. Second, turn the large red dial labelled *Genetic Manipulation Method* to the setting *Hatch*.

3. When you set the dial to *Hatch*, all of the slots on the *Input Creatures* bin of the Genetic Manipulator will close.

4. Press the black *Activate* button. A hatched creature of the sort matching the egg you provided will appear in the *Output Creature* bin of the Genetic Manipulator.

How to Log the Hatching of a Logibeast: Hatching a beast directly from an egg barely counts as a "recipe" for creating a beast, but we'll start with logging a simple hatching, just to introduce the basic elements of beast logging. You'll notice that each page of your Genetic Logbook contains a bunch of lines divided into five columns. At the top of each page the five columns are labelled as follows:

Eggs	Step	Genetic Method	Input Creatures	Output Creature

Let's go through the significance of each of these columns:

2.1. A BRIEF INTRODUCTION TO LOGIBEAST GENETIC RECIPES

1. **Eggs**: In this column, you will list the eggs needed to create (and sustain) the creature being created in the current genetic manipulation step. In hatching a Fluftoom, we will need a Fluftoom egg. (No big surprise there, but when we start creating more advanced and exotic creatures, the needed eggs will be less predictable.)

2. **Step**: In this column, we just keep track of the step number in the genetic manipulation sequence. Since hatching a Fluftoom is a single step procedure, there will be only one line, and that line will be Step 1.

3. **Method**: In this column, we indicate what setting we want on the Genetic Manipulation Method dial for this step in the process. For hatching a Fluftoom, we want the Hatch method. We'll learn about other methods later.

4. **Input Creatures**: In this column, we indicate what creatures we need to place in the Input Creatures bin for the selected genetic manipulation method to use in creating our new creature. The Hatch method doesn't require any prior creatures, so for hatching a Fluftoom, this column is empty.

5. **Output Creature**: In this column, we indicate what creature appears in the Output Creature bin of the Genetic Manipulator in this step of the process. When hatching a Fluftoom, it's a Fluftoom that will appear in the Output Creature bin.

So here's the very short recipe for hatching a Fluftoom:

Eggs	Step	Genetic Method	Input Creatures	Output Creature
(Fluftoom)	1	Hatch	-	Fluftoom

Once you get more familiar with the various Logibeasts, it's often more convenient to write the recipes with pictures of the beasts, rather than with names, like this:

Eggs	Step	Genetic Method	Input Creatures	Output Creature
(🐾)	1	Hatch	-	🐾

In this guide we'll present recipes in both styles (texts and pictures) to let you get used to both.

2.2 Grotesque Merge and Split

How to Make a Grotesque Logibeast: So, now you've hatched your very own Fluftoom. Wasn't that fun? But at some point you're going to want to create something a bit more formidable than a fluffy little Fluftoom.

Any two Logibeasts can be genetically spliced into a single Grotesque beast. Let's see how to combine an Oolopod and a Yttrig into a Grotesque beast. If you consult the Logibestiary in the appendix to this guide, you'll find that the genetic combination of an Oolopod and a Yttrig creates a Grotesque Ogrit. But what's the actual procedure for producing the Grotesque Ogrit?
Well, here's the recipe:

Eggs	Step	Genetic Method	Input Creatures	Output Creature
(Oolopod)	1	Hatch	-	Oolopod
(Yttrig)	2	Hatch	-	Yttrig
(Oolopod, Yttrig)	3	Grotesque Merge	1,2	Grotesque Ogrit

Or, pictorially:

Eggs	Step	Genetic Method	Input Creatures	Output Creature
(🐑)	1	Hatch	-	🐑
(🐎)	2	Hatch	-	🐎
(🐑, 🐎)	3	Grotesque Merge	1,2	🐾

Let's go through this a step at a time to make sure we understand how everything is working.

1. First, place an Oolopod egg in the egg receptacle and set the dial to Hatch. Press the button, and you've got yourself a live Oolopod. (Careful not to let the slime get everywhere!)

2. Take the Oolopod out of the genetic manipulator and set it aside. Now put a Yttrig egg in the receptacle, make sure the dial is still on Hatch, and press the button again. Now you've also got a cute little Yttrig.

3. Now it's time to use the Grotesque Merge method. Turn the Genetic Manipulation Method dial to the Grotesque Merge method. Notice that two slots open in the Input Creatures bin. That's because Grotesque Merge takes two creatures and combines them into a new one. Place the Oolopod in the first slot and the Yttrig in the second slot.

2.2. GROTESQUE MERGE AND SPLIT

Notice that on the third line of the recipe, under *Input Creatures*, we don't list in detail that an Oolopd and a Yttrig are being used as input. Instead, we just put '1,2', meaning that the creatures created in steps 1 and 2 of the recipe are now used as inputs. That's just a way to save a little space in writing up your recipe.

4. With the dial set and the Oolopod and Yttrig in place, press the button, step back, and behold (if you dare) your brand-new Grotesque Ogrit.

5. Finally, let's say something about eggs. Notice that step 3 of the recipe indicates that the Grotesque Ogrit requires both the Oolopod and the Yttrig egg to be created, and to remain alive. That's a general feature of Grotesque Merge: *when you combine two creatures with Grotesque Merge, the resulting creature depends on the combination of all of the eggs that the two input creatures individually depended on.*

Grotesque Merge can be used to combine *any* two Logibeasts into a new Grotesque beast. For example, we can combine a Grotesque Ogrit with an Eldritch Whylxot. (Your Logibeast starter kit doesn't come with any Eldritch eggs. However, you can purchase at any Logibeast store egg expansion sets, each of which is guaranteed to contain at least one Eldritch egg.) Here's the recipe:

Eggs	Step	Genetic Method	Input Creatures	Output Creature
(Grotesque Ogrit)	1	Hatch	-	Grotesque Ogrit
(Eldritch Whylxot)	2	Hatch	-	Eldritch Whylxot
(Grotesque Ogrit, Eldritch Whylxot)	3	Grotesque Merge	1,2	Grotesque Uuhulmo

Or pictorially:

Eggs	Step	Genetic Method	Input Creatures	Output Creature
(🐾)	1	Hatch	-	🐾
( )	2	Hatch	-	
(🐾 ,)	3	Grotesque Merge	1,2	🐉

Okay, let's wrap up this little introduction to Grotesque Merge with a brief summary of how Grotesque Merge works:

Grotesque Merge:

- Input: any two creatures

32   *CHAPTER 2. LOGIBEAST GENETIC ENGINEERING*

- Output: Grotesque Merge of the two input creatures
- Eggs: combined eggs of the two input creatures

How to Use a Grotesque Logibeast: Hatch and Grotesque Merge are just the beginning of the many exciting options on the Genetic Manipulation Method dial. Let's move on to another choice: the Grotesque Split. Turn the dial to Grotesque Split. You'll see that there's now only one open slot in the Input bin. That's beecause Grotesque Split, unlike Grotesque Merge, takes only one creature as input. An initial word of warning: Grotesque Split can only be used if you already have a Grotesque creature to put in the Input bin. Try running Grotesque Split on anything other than a Grotesque creature (a Primeval creature, for example, or even worse a Winged creature), and you're going to end up with a fizzled genetic experiment, a nasty mess to clean up, and a thoroughly voided warranty.

But if you do have a Grotesque creature around, Grotesque Split allows you to extract some of its genes and derive a new creature from it. To see what new creature can be made with Grotesque Split, consult the Logibestiary. Find the Grotesque creature you have on hand, and read back across the arrow to see what two creatures combine (via Grotesque Merge) to make that creature. Either one of those can be created using Grotesque Split. Here's a sample recipe:

Eggs	Step	Genetic Method	Input Creatures	Output Creature
(Grotesque Ogrit)	1	Hatch	-	Grotesque Ogrit
(Grotesque Ogrit)	2	Grotesque Split	1	Yttrig

Or pictorially:

Eggs	Step	Genetic Method	Input Creatures	Output Creature
(🐾)	1	Hatch	-	🐾
(🐾)	2	Grotesque Split	1	🐾

Notice that if you make your Yttrig this way, rather than hatching it directly from a Yttrig egg, then it's dependent on the Grotesque Ogrit egg, rather than on a Yttrig egg.

By combining Grotesque Merge and Grotesque Split, you can create all sort of exciting new creatures. Suppose you've got hold of

2.3. PRIMEVAL MERGE AND SPLIT

a Grotesque Uuhulmo egg. Then you can tinker away to create a Grotesque Hjunklit:

Eggs	Step	Genetic Method	Input Creatures	Output Creature
(Grotesque Uuhulmo)	1	Hatch	-	Grotesque Uuhulmo
(Grotesque Uuhulmo)	2	Grotesque Split	1	Grotesque Ogrit
(Grotesque Uuhulmo)	3	Grotesque Split	1	Eldritch Whylxot
(Grotesque Uuhulmo)	4	Grotesque Split	2	Oolopod
(Grotesque Uuhulmo)	5	Grotesque Merge	3,4	Grotesque Hjunkit

Or pictorially:

Eggs	Step	Genetic Method	Input Creatures	Output Creature
(🙲)	1	Hatch	-	🙲
(🙲)	2	Grotesque Split	1	🙲
(🙲)	3	Grotesque Split	1	
(🙲)	4	Grotesque Split	2	🙲
(🙲)	5	Grotesque Merge	3,4	🙲

Here's the brief summary of how Grotesque Split works:

Grotesque Split:

- Input: any Grotesque creature
- Output: either mother or father of the Grotesque creature
- Eggs: eggs of the input Grotesque creature

2.3 Primeval Merge and Split

How to Use a Primeval Logibeast: Grotesque creatures are great, but the grotesque doesn't exhaust the Logibeast world. Let's talk next about Primeval creatures. Like Grotesque creatures, Primeval creatures can be used to make new beasts. But the genetics of Primeval creatures are a bit more complicated, so we need to learn a new procedure. Suppose you've gotten hold of an egg for a Primeval Schniftoo. Consulting the Logibestiary, you discover that the Primeval Schniftoo in the wild is the offspring of a Fluftoom mother and an Aarobak father. (Remember that for Primeval creatures, unlike Grotesque creatures, the roles of mother and father in ancestry matter.) In that case, if you've got a Fluftoom around already, you can use your Primeval Schniftoo to create an Aarobak. Just set the Genetic Manipulation Method dial to *Primeval Split*, put the Primeval Schniftoo and the Fluftoom in the two slots of the Input bin (be sure to put the Primeval Schniftoo in the first slot!), and press the button. Here's the recipe:

Eggs	Step	Genetic Method	Input Creatures	Output Creature
(Primeval Schniftoo)	1	Hatch	-	Primeval Schniftoo
(Fluftoom)	2	Hatch	-	Fluftoom
(Primeval Schniftoo, Fluftoom)	3	Primeval Split	1,2	Aarobak

Or pictorially:

Eggs	Step	Genetic Method	Input Creatures	Output Creature
()	1	Hatch	-	
( )	2	Hatch	-	
(,)	3	Primeval Split	1,2	

Remember, don't try to use Primeval Split if you don't have a Primeval creature in the first slot of the Input Bin. If you do, you'll end up with no new Logibeast, and a horrid stench of burnt beast filling your laboratory. (And, once more, a voided warranty.) Also, be sure you put the *mother* of the Primeval creature in the other slot of the Input bin. If you put in the father, or some other unrelated Logibeast, you're pretty much guaranteed to short out the central genetic filter of the Manipulator, and you definitely won't end up with a new beast.

Here's the brief summary of how Primeval Split works:

Primeval Split:
- Input: any Primeval creature and its mother
- Output: father of the Primeval creature
- Eggs: combined eggs of the two input creatures

How to Make a Primeval Logibeast: Making a Primeval beast isn't quite as straightforward as making a Grotesque beast, but with practice, you can use your Genetic Manipulator to turn out a wide variety of exciting (and sometimes quite dangerous, so be careful!) Primeval beasts. You can even make Primeval beasts that don't require any eggs at all – that's a trick that just can't be turned with Grotesque beasts.

2.3. PRIMEVAL MERGE AND SPLIT

To make a Primeval beast, you'll want to set the Genetic Manipulation Method to *Primeval Merge*. But before you do that, you" first need to have made the mother and the father of the Primeval beast you're trying for. (As usual, consult the Logibestiary for details on what the parents of a given Primeval beast are.) For example, suppose you want to make your own Primeval Knug. A Primeval Knug has a Schloof as a mother and a Yttrig as a father, so you'll need to create one of each of these. But there is a very important constraint:

- When using Primeval Merge, the *mother* of the Primeval beast you are creating needs to be **newly hatched**. The mother can't have been created through any genetic method other than a direct hatching. Any other method introduces quantum irregularities in the genetic structure of the mother that always cause the Primeval Merge to fail.

With that warning in place, let's look at a simple recipe for a Primeval Knug:

Eggs	Step	Genetic Method	Input Creatures	Output Creature
(Schloof)	1	Hatch	-	Schloof
(Yttrig)	2	Hatch	-	Yttrig
(Schloof)	3	Primeval Merge	1,2	Primeval Knug

Or pictorially:

Eggs	Step	Genetic Method	Input Creatures	Output Creature
(🐾)	1	Hatch	-	🐾
(🐾)	2	Hatch	-	🐾
(🐾)	3	Primeval Merge	1,2	🐾

We know what you're thinking: *Hey, Logibeast people! You made a big mistake in that last recipe. Look at the eggs on the third line – you forgot to include the Schloof egg used to hatch the Schloof that's the mother of the Primeval Knug!* But that's one of the amazing things about Primeval beasts – they don't depend on eggs in exactly the same way that Grotesque beasts do. In particular:

- When you use Primeval Merge on a (newly hatched) mother beast and. a father beast to create a Primeval beast, the newly created Primeval beast needs the *father's* eggs, but not the mother's eggs.

Nothing against mothers – they're great, and we here at Logibeast™ Central all recognize our dependence on our own – but when it comes to the Primeval beasts, they really cut the apron strings and don't depend on their mothers at all.

Let's look at one slightly more complicated example of building a Primeval beast. Suppose you've got hold of a Primeval Quiffex egg. (Oh, look – we've actually been able to provide a Primeval Quiffex egg in the standard starter kit, thanks to the generosity of our new Primeval supplier.) Then you can build yourself a Primeval Knug using the following recipe:

Eggs	Step	Genetic Method	Input Creatures	Output Creature
(Primeval Quiffex)	1	Hatch	-	Primeval Quiffex
(Schloof)	2	Hatch	-	Schloof
(Primeval Quiffex, Schloof)	3	Primeval Split	1,2	Grotesque Ogrit
(Primeval Quiffex, Schloof)	4	Grotesque Split	3	Yttrig
(Primeval Quiffex)	5	Primeval Merge	2,4	Primeval Knug

Or pictorially:

Eggs	Step	Genetic Method	Input Creatures	Output Creature
(🐾)	1	Hatch	-	🐾
(🐾)	2	Hatch	-	🐾
(🐾, 🐾)	3	Primeval Split	1,2	🐾
(🐾, 🐾)	4	Grotesque Split	3	🐾
(🐾)	5	Primeval Merge	2,4	🐾

Notice that although you use a Schloof egg to create the Primeval Knug, the final Knug doesn't actually depend on the Schloof egg, so if you lose your Schloof egg, it won't endanger the Primeval Knug.

We mentioned earlier that you can create Primeval beasts that are completely egg-independent, so let's give a quick example of that. Suppose you've got an Oolopod egg. Then you can use the following recipe:

Eggs	Step	Genetic Method	Input Creatures	Output Creature
(Oolopod)	1	Hatch	-	Oolopod
-	2	Primeval Merge	1,1	Primeval Protopod

Or pictorially:

2.4. WINGED MERGE AND SPLIT

Eggs	Step	Genetic Method	Input Creatures	Output Creature
(🐛)	1	Hatch	-	🐛
-	2	Primeval Merge	1,1	🐛

And you've got yourself a Primeval Protopod. Notice that your newly-hatched Oolopod plays both mother and father role for the Primeval Protopod. (You really don't want to know the details.) That means that the Oolopod goes in *both* slots in the Input bin. Don't worry – they're surprisingly stretchable.

Here's the brief summary of how Primeval Merge works:

Primeval Merge:

- Input: any two creatures – one to play the role of mother of a Primeval creature; the other to play the role of father. The mother input creature must be newly hatched.

- Output: Primeval Merge of the two input creatures

- Eggs: eggs of the father creature, minus the egg of the mother creature (if it was included in the eggs of the father creature)

2.4 Winged Merge and Split

How to Use a Winged Logibeast: Once you've mastered working with Primeval beasts, you're ready to move on to Winged beasts. They're very similar to Primeval beasts in many way. But there's one important difference. For Primeval beasts, it matters which beast is mother and which beast is father. But for Winged beasts (as with Grotesque beasts), it doesn't matter. An Aarobak mother and an Oolopod father can give birth to a Winged Hvornid, but also an Oolopod mother and an Aarobak father can give birth to a Winged Hvornid. Winged beasts, as we'll see, then are basically like Primeval beasts with the mother+father difference erased.

Set your Genetic Manipulation Method dial to *Winged Split*. If you then put a Winged beast in the first slot of the Input bin and the mother of that beast in the second slot, you can get the father of the Winged beast in the Output bin. Or put the Winged beast and

38   CHAPTER 2. LOGIBEAST GENETIC ENGINEERING

its *father* in the Input bin, and get its *mother* in the Output bin. It's entirely up to you!

(The usual **warnings** apply. Don't try to use Winged Split without a Winged beast in the first slot of the input bin, and don't try to put anything other than mother or father of that beast in the second Input slot. A number of very clear court decisions have established that we are *not* responsible for any genetic abnormalities in you the user, or in your children, that result from ignoring these warnings.)

Here's a quick example:

Eggs	Step	Genetic Method	Input Creatures	Output Creature
(Winged Xeerun)	1	Hatch	-	Winged Xeerun
(Fluftoom)	2	Hatch	-	Fluftoom
(Winged Xeerun, Fluftoom)	3	Winged Split	1,2	Oolopod

Or pictorially:

Eggs	Step	Genetic Method	Input Creatures	Output Creature
(🜋)	1	Hatch	-	🜋
(⚬)	2	Hatch	-	⚬
(🜋 , ⚬)	3	Winged Split	1,2	🝙

Here we have split the Winged Xeerun using its mother to create its father. A more complicated example:

Eggs	Step	Genetic Method	Input Creatures	Output Creature
(Winged Hvornid)	1	Hatch	-	Winged Hvornid
(Aarobak)	2	Hatch	-	Aarobak
(Winged Hvornid, Aarobak)	3	Winged Split	1,2	Oolopod
(Winged Hvornid)	4	Primeval Merge	2,3	Primeval Gtuftbak
(Oolopod)	5	Hatch	-	Oolopod
(Winged Hvornid, Oolopod)	6	Wingedn Split	1,5	Aarobak
(Winged Hvornid)	7	Primeval Merge	5,6	Primeval J'jaklu
(Winged Hvornid)	8	Grotesque Merge	4,7	Grotesque Qeqesflon

Or, pictorially:

2.4. WINGED MERGE AND SPLIT

Eggs	Step	Genetic Method	Input Creatures	Output Creature
( )	1	Hatch	-	
( )	2	Hatch	-	
(,)	3	Winged Split	1,2	
( )	4	Primeval Merge	2,3	
( )	5	Hatch	-	
(,)	6	Winged Split	1,5	
( )	7	Primeval Merge	5,6	
( )	8	Grotesque Merge	4,7	

In this bit of genetic manipulation, we start with a Winged Hvornid. By hatching an Aarobak, we can extract an Oolopod from the Winged Hvornid, and then combine the Aarobak and the Oolopod to make a Primeval Gtuftbak. Next we hatch an Oolobak and again use the Winged Hvornid, this time to extract an Aarobak. (The first time we use the mother to extract the father; this time we use the father to extract the mother.) From an Oolopod and an Aarobak, we can make a Primeval J'jaklu. (Notice that we couldn't use the Oolopod created in step 3 – we needed a freshly hatched Oolopod.) Finally, a quick Grotesque Merge of the Primeval Gtuftbak and the Primeval J'jaklu gives us the much-prized Grotesque Qeqesflon.

Here's the brief summary of how Winged Split works:

Winged Split:
- Input: a Winged creature and either the mother or the father of that Winged creature.
- Output: either the father or the mother of the input Winged creature (depending on whether the mother or the father was input)
- Eggs: combined eggs of the two input creatures

How to Make a Winged Logibeast: Making a Winged Logibeast is kind of like making a Primeval Logibeast twice over. To make a Primeval Logibeast, you hatch its mother, make its father, and then merge them. To make a Winged Logibeast, you hatch its mother and make its father, and then you hatch its *father* and make its *mother*, and then you merge all of that.

Let's look at an example. Suppose you have a Oolopod egg, and you want to make a Winged Shugraat. The mother of a Winged Shugraat is a Yttrig, and the father of a Winged Shugraat is a Grotesque Ogrit. So you need to do two things:

1. Hatch a Yttrig and make a Grotesque Ogrit

2. Hatch a Grotesque Ogrit and make a Yttrig

Then you'll need to set that dial to Winged Merge, put everything together, and out will pop your Winged Shugraat. (And they really do pop, so stand back when pressing the final button.)

Here's the recipe:

Eggs	Step	Genetic Method	Input Creatures	Output Creature
(Oolopod)	1	Hatch	-	Oolopod
(Yttrig)	2	Hatch	-	Yttrig
(Yttrig, Oolopod)	3	Grotesque Merge	1,2	Grotesque Ogrit
(Grotesque Ogrit)	4	Hatch	-	Grotesque Ogrit
(Grotesque Ogrit)	5	Grotesque Split	4	Yttrig
(Oolopod)	6	Winged Merge	2,3,4,5	Winged Shugraat

Or pictorially:

Eggs	Step	Genetic Method	Input Creatures	Output Creature
(🐑)	1	Hatch	-	🐑
(🐐)	2	Hatch	-	🐐
(🐐 , 🐑)	3	Grotesque Merge	1,2	🐎
(🐎)	4	Hatch	-	🐎
(🐎)	5	Grotesque Split	4	🐐
(🐑)	6	Winged Merge	2,3,4,5	🐕

Most of this recipe is straightforward. In steps 2 and 3, we hatch the mother of the Winged Shugraat (the Yttrig) and build its father (the Grotesque Ogrit). In steps 4 and 5, we hatch the father of the Winged Shugraat (the Grotesque Ogrit) and build its mother (the Yttrig). Then in the sixth and final step, we merge the two Yttrigs and the two Grotesque Ogrits from steps 2 through 5 to make our Winged Shugrat. But what's going on with the eggs? Why does

2.4. WINGED MERGE AND SPLIT

our final Winged Shugraat need only the *Oolopod* egg?

Remember that when you are building a Primeval creature with Primeval Merge, you *remove* the dependency on the mother's egg when you make the Primeval creature. The Primeval creature is mother-independent – it relies on whatever its father relied on, except the mother's egg. It's the same idea for the Winged beast, but in both directions. The Winged beast relies on whatever eggs its unhatched father needs, minus its hatched mother's egg, and *also* on whatever eggs its unhatched mother needs, minus its hatched father's egg.

In this case, the unhatched father is the Grotesque Ogrit of the third step, which relies on a Yttrig and an Oolopod egg. And the unhatched mother is the Yttrig of the fifth step, which relies on a Grotesque Ogrit egg. So that's a total of a Yttrig, an Oolopod, and a Grotesque Ogrit egg. We then remove from that list the eggs of the hatched mother and the hatched father. That's a Yttrig egg (mother) and a Grotesque Ogrit egg (father). Only an Oolopod egg remains.

Who would have guessed that with just the egg of a lowly Oolopod, you could grow yourself a mighty Winged Shugraat? That's only the beginning of the many marvels of Logibeast genetic engineering.

Here's the brief summary of how Winged Merge works:

Winged Merge:

- Input: Four creatures: a newly-hatched mother of the Winged creature, a father of the Winged creature, a newly hatched father of the Winged creature, and a mother of the Winged creature

- Output: the Winged creature whose mother and father are the input creatures

- Eggs: the combined eggs of the (unhatched) mother and father, minus the eggs of the hatched mother and the hatched father

42 CHAPTER 2. LOGIBEAST GENETIC ENGINEERING

2.5 Bloodthirsty Merge and Split

How to Make a Bloodthirsty Logibeast: By now you're getting to be quite the expert in Logibeast genetic engineering. You should be able to manipulate Grotesque, Primeval, and Winged beasts to make all sorts of fascinating and terrifying creatures. But you're not yet a total master – we still need to learn about Bloodthirsty and Eldritch beasts. We'll start with the fine art of making Bloodthirsty beasts.

The peculiar genetic structure of Bloodthirsty beasts makes them very easy to create in the laboratory. If you have *either* the mother *or* the father of a Bloodthirsty beast on hand, just set the Genetic Manipulation Method dial to *Bloodthirsty Merge*, drop the mother+father in the slot of the Input bin (notice that only one slot will be open once you've set the dial to Bloodthirsty Merge), and press the big black button.

Here's a sample recipe (a short one, since Bloodthirsty Merges are so easy):

Eggs	Step	Genetic Method	Input Creatures	Output Creature
(Oolopod)	1	Hatch	-	Oolopod
(Oolopod)	2	Bloodthirsty Merge	1	Bloodthirsty Awtroof

Or pictorially:

Eggs	Step	Genetic Method	Input Creatures	Output Creature
(🐾)	1	Hatch	-	🐾
(🐾)	2	Bloodthirsty Merge	1	🐾

No need for a Fluftoom in making your Bloodthirsty Awtroof – the mother Oolopod is enough. But if you happen to have a Fluftoom egg instead of an Oolopod egg, that will also do the job:

Eggs	Step	Genetic Method	Input Creatures	Output Creature
(Fluftoom)	1	Hatch	-	Fluftoom
(Fluftoom)	2	Bloodthirsty Merge	1	Bloodthirsty Awtroof

Or pictorially:

Eggs	Step	Genetic Method	Input Creatures	Output Creature
(⊙)	1	Hatch	-	🐾
(⊙)	2	Bloodthirsty Merge	1	🐾

2.5. BLOODTHIRSTY MERGE AND SPLIT

Here's an example of a more complicated bit of genetic engineering that uses Bloodthirsty Merge along the way. Suppose you've got an egg for a Primeval Vringxed. (These have been showing up on LogiBay at great prices recently, usually in excellent condition.) With a bit of work, you can actually extract a Primeval Schniftoo from that egg. Here's the recipe:

Eggs	Step	Genetic Method	Input Creatures	Output Creature
(Primeval Vringxed)	1	Hatch	-	Primeval Vringxed
(Fluftoom)	2	Hatch	-	Fluftoom
(Fluftoom)	3	Bloodthirsty Merge	2	Bloodthirsty Awtroof
(Fluftoom, Primeval Vringxed)	4	Primeval Split	2,3	Aarobak
(Primeval Vringxed)	5	Primeval Merge	2,4	Primeval Schniftoo

Or pictorially:

Eggs	Step	Genetic Method	Input Creatures	Output Creature
()	1	Hatch	-	
( )	2	Hatch	-	
( )	3	Bloodthirrsty Merge	2	
(,)	4	Primeval Split	2,3	
()	5	Primeval Merge	2,4	

Here's the brief summary of how Bloodthirsty Merge works:

Bloodthirsty Merge:
- Input: any creature
- Output: a Bloodthirsty creature having the input creature as either mother or father
- Eggs: the eggs of the input creature

How to Use a Bloodthirsty Logibeast: Bloodthirsty beasts are easy to create through genetic engineering, but they're somewhat trickier to make use of in doing further engineering. Still, with a bit of practice, you'll soon be tossing Bloodthirsty beasts into those input bins and making even more exotic beasts.

Let's just leap right into an example. Suppose you want to make a Grotesque Ogrit. That would be easy if you happened to have an Oolopod egg and a Yttrig egg, of course – just hatch both and then do a quick Grotesque Merge. But you don't. You do have a Yttrig egg, but no Oolopod egg. In addition, you've got a Primeval Quiffex egg and a Bloodthirsty Cavaidko egg.

44 CHAPTER 2. LOGIBEAST GENETIC ENGINEERING

A Bloodthirsty Cavaidko has an Oolopod and a Schloof as parents. What we're going to do is make our desired Grotesque Ogrit from each of the parents. Then we can throw everything into a big Bloodthirsty Merge blender, and out will come a Grotesque Ogrit made from the Bloodthirsty Cavaidko. Here's how the details go:

Eggs	Step	Genetic Method	Input Creatures	Output Creature
(Bloodthirsty Cavaidko)	1	Hatch	-	Bloodthirsty Cavaidko
(Yttrig)	2	Hatch	-	Yttrig
(Primeval Quiffex)	3	Hatch	-	Primeval Quiffex
(Oolopod)	4	Hatch	-	Oolopod
(Oolopod, Yttrig)	5	Grotesque Merge	3,4	Grotesque Ogrit
(Schloof)	6	Hatch	-	Schloof
(Schloof, Primeval Quiffex)	7	Primeval Split	3,6	Grotesque Ogrit
(Yttrig, Primeval Quiffex, Bloodthirstt Cavaidko)	8	Bloodthirsty Split	1,4,5,6,7	Grotesque Ogrit

Or pictorially:

Eggs	Step	Genetic Method	Input Creatures	Output Creature
( )	1	Hatch	-	
( )	2	Hatch	-	
( )	3	Hatch	-	
( )	4	Hatch	-	
(,)	5	Grotesque Merge	3,4	
( )	6	Hatch	-	
(,)	7	Primeval Split	3,6	
(, ,)	8	Bloodthirsty Split	1,4,5,6,7	

Now let's get clear on what just happened. In step 4 we hatched an Oolopod, the father of a Bloodthirsty Cavaidko. Then in the fifth step we used the Oolopod to make a Grotesque Ogrit, by merging it with a Yttrig we happened to have on hand.

In step 6 we then hatched a Schloof, the mother of a Bloodthirsty Cavaidko. In the seventh step we then used the Schloof to make *another* Grotesque Ogrit, this time by splitting with a Primeval Quiffex we had around.

At this point we've made two Grotesque Ogrits. But neither of them is what we wanted, because we've made them with the wrong eggs. The two Grotesque Ogrits we've made rely on Oolopod and Schloof eggs (respectively) that we don't have to spare.

2.5. BLOODTHIRSTY MERGE AND SPLIT

So the last step is to make one more Grotesque Ogrit. This one depends not on the Oolopod or on the Schloof, but rather on the Bloodthirsty Cavaidko that has the Oolopod and the Schloof as parents. So we get rid of the reliance on the Oolopod and Schloof eggs, and replace them with a reliance on the Bloodthirsty Cavaidko egg.

Here's the brief summary of how Bloodthirsty Split works:

Bloodthirsty Split:

- Input: *Five* creatures: a Bloodthirsty creature, a newly hatched mother and a newly hatched father of the Bloodthirsty creature, and some other creature made twice over, once using the newly-hatched mother and once using the newly-hatched father
- Output: The creature input twice over
- Eggs: The combined eggs of the two instances of the output creature in the input bin, plus the eggs of the Bloodthirsty creature in the input bin, minus the eggs of the newly-hatched mother and father

Bloodthirsty Split is definitely the trickiest of the genetic methods, so don't feel bad if it takes you a few tries to get it working right, and if you end up with some hideous genetic anomalies along the way. (We've even thoughtfully built in some safeguards to the Genetic Manipulator to prevent repeats of some of the more gruesome mishaps that haunted the early attempts at Bloodthirsty Split.) Some things to keep in mind:

1. Whenever you do a Bloodthirsty Split, you're going to build the same creature *three times* over the course of your experiment. Once you'll build it from a starting point of the mother of your Bloodthirsty beast; once you'll build it from the father of your Bloodthirsty beast; and then at the end you'll build it directly from your Bloodthirsty beast. Don't get discouraged because you are doing the same thing – you really are making progress toward your final goal. And keep track of where you are in the process. You don't want to forget, and end up treating your second round of creation as if it were the final round.

2. Remember that you're going to need a total of five creatures for the Input bin for Bloodthirsty Split. That's more than any other genetic method. It's also a lot to keep track of, but there's a very simple structure for those five:

   - One Bloodthirsty creature
   - Both the mother and the father of that Bloodthirsty creature, both newly hatched
   - Two copies of some other creature – that's then the creature that will emerge in the Output bin.

3. And in the midst of all of that, don't lose track of the fact that the mother and the father of the Bloodthirsty creature need to be newly hatched, just like with Primeval Merge and Winged Merge. Don't try to use a mother or father that you've built through your own genetic manipulations. Our safeguards will detect this, the warning siren will sound, and the Genetic Manipulator will seal itself and await arrival of a Logibeast™ inspector to reset the matrix.

2.6 Eldritch Merge and Split

How to Use an Eldritch Logibeast: Okay, we're almost done now. All that remains is the strange world of Eldritch beasts. Remember, Eldritch beasts are produced in the wild through parthenogenesis, so unlike other beasts, they have only one parent, rather than two. The Genetic Manipulator offers two methods for dealing with Eldritch beasts. As with the other beast families, there is a split method (Eldritch Split) and a merge method (Eldritch Merge).

Let's start with Eldritch Split. This method is very easy – there's only one important thing to keep in mind. Eldritch Split, applied to an Eldritch creature, returns the Eldritch *grandparent* of that Eldritch creature. For example, the parent of an Eldritch Mumfloom is an Eldritch Webblob, and the parent of an Eldritch Webblob is an Aarobak. (As usual, facts like this we get by consulting the Logibestiary.) So the Aarobak is the Eldritch grandparent of an Eldritch Mumfloom. That means that if we set the dial to Eldritch Split, put an Eldritch Mumfloom into the Input bin (which will have only one open slot), out will come an Aarobak in the Output bin.

2.6. ELDRITCH MERGE AND SPLIT

Why does Eldritch Split produce the Eldritch *grandparent* of a creature, rather than its Eldritch parent? This was a central question of Logibeast research for almost 30 years, until the advent of Generalized Eldritch Field Theory in the 1970s made it clear that the cyclic quaternion pattern to the Myxmar Eldritch wave function allowed real-valued solutions only every other generation. Still, that's the kind of stuff for specialists to worry about, not the concern of the work-a-day Logibeast engineer. All you need to know is to expect those grandparents to be emerging.

Because Eldritch Split is so simple, there's not much to the recipes, but here's one just to make sure you see how the details go:

Eggs	Step	Genetic Method	Input Creatures	Output Creature
(Eldritch Mumfloom)	1	Hatch	-	Eldritch Mumfloom
(Eldritch Mumfloom)	2	Eldritch Split	1	Aarobak

Or pictorially:

Eggs	Step	Genetic Method	Input Creatures	Output Creature
()	1	Hatch	-	
()	2	Eldritch Split	1	🐉

And here is the brief summary of how Eldritch Split works:

Eldritch Split:

- Input: an Eldritch creature whose parent is also an Eldritch creature
- Output: the Eldritch grandparent of the input creature
- Eggs: the eggs of the input creature

How to Make an Eldritch Logibeast: There's only one setting left to explore on the Genetic Manipulation Method dial: *Eldritch Merge*. Eldritch Merge is used to produce the Eldritch *offspring* of a newly hatched creature. To extract that Eldritch offspring, you need along the way to create some creature and *its* Eldritch offspring. ('Eldritch makes Eldritch', as the saying goes.)

Here's a sample recipe using Eldritch Merge:

48   CHAPTER 2. LOGIBEAST GENETIC ENGINEERING

Eggs	Step	Genetic Method	Input Creatures	Output Creature
(Aarobak)	1	Hatch	-	Aarobak
(Primeval Gtuftbak)	2	Hatch	-	Primeval Gtuftbak
(Eldritch Iumhfiss)	3	Hatch	-	Eldritch Iumhfiss
(Aarobak, Primeval Gtuftbak)	4	Primeval Split	1,2	Oolopod
(Primeval Gtuftbak, Eldritch Iumhfiss)	5	Eldritch Merge	1,3,4	Eldritch Webblob

Or pictorially:

Eggs	Step	Genetic Method	Input Creatures	Output Creature
(🝔)	1	Hatch	-	🝔
(🝕)	2	Hatch	-	🝕
(🝖)	3	Hatch	-	🝖
(🝔, 🝕)	4	Primeval Split	1,2	🝗
(🝕, 🝖)	5	Eldritch Merge	1,3,4	🝘

This recipe takes us from an Aarobak to its Eldritch offspring the Eldritch Webblob. To get there, we need to produce another creature+Eldritch offspring pair. We do this by being fortunate enough to have an Eldritch Iumhfiss egg sitting around, and then noticing that the Eldritch Iumhfiss is the Eldritch offspring of the Oolopod, and finally noticing that we can get an Oolopod from the Primeval Gtuftbak we have available, since the Aarobak is the Primeval Gtuftbak's mother.

As with most of our other merge methods (Primeval Merge, Winged Merge, and Bloodthirsty Merge), it's crucial that we use newly-hatched creatures in the right places. With Eldritch Merge, it's the Logibeast that's the parent of our target Eldritch creature that needs to be newly hatched.

Notice how the eggs work with Eldritch Merge. To complete the Eldritch Merge, we need to produce another pair of creature+Eldritch offspring. We then gather up all of the eggs needed to make that pair. (In the recipe we just considered, that's an Eldritch Iumhfiss egg (for the Eldritch Iumhfiss) and Aarobak and Primeval Gtuftbak eggs (for the Oolopod). We then *remove* from that collection of eggs the egg from which we hatched the parent of the target Eldritch creature. (In our above recipe, that means we don't need the Aarobak egg anymore once we have our Eldritch Webblob.) The Eldritch offspring *rejects its parent*, and is dependent on everything *but* the parent.

Here's the brief summary of how Eldritch Merge works:

Eldritch Merge:
- Input: a newly-hatched creature (the parent of the target Eldritch creature), and another creature and its Eldritch offspring
- Output: the Eldritch offspring of the first input creature
- Eggs: the combined eggs of the creature+Eldritch offspring pair in the input, minus the egg of the newly-hatched parent of the output Eldritch creature

And that's it – that's all of the Logibeast genetic manipulation methods. You are now a master Logibeast genetic engineer. Have at it, and see what strange and wonderful creations you can add to the Logibeast world!

2.7 Brief Review of the Genetic Methods

There are a total of eleven settings on your Genetic Methods dial. Here is a quick chart of all eleven and how to use them.

Hatch	<ul><li>Input: None</li><li>Output: Creature hatched from the egg</li><li>Eggs: Egg of the hatched creature</li></ul>
Grotesque Split	<ul><li>Input: any Grotesque creature</li><li>Output: either mother or father of the Grotesque creature</li><li>Eggs: eggs of the input Grotesque creature</li></ul>
Grotesque Merge	<ul><li>Input: any two creatures</li><li>Output: Grotesque Merge of the two input creatures</li><li>Eggs: combined eggs of the two input creatures</li></ul>

Primeval Split	<ul><li>Input: any Primeval creature and its mother</li><li>Output: father of the Primeval creature</li><li>Eggs: combined eggs of the two input creatures</li></ul>
Primeval Merge	<ul><li>Input: any two creatures – one to play the role of mother of a Primeval creature; the other to play the role of father. The mother input creature must be newly hatched.</li><li>Output: Primeval Merge of the two input creatures</li><li>Eggs: eggs of the father creature, minus the egg of the mother creature (if it was included in the eggs of the father creature)</li></ul>
Winged Split	<ul><li>Input: a Winged creature and either the mother or the father of that Winged creature.</li><li>Output: either the father or the mother of the input Winged creature (depending on whether the mother or the father was input)</li><li>Eggs: combined eggs of the two input creatures</li></ul>
Winged Merge	<ul><li>Input: Four creatures: a newly-hatched mother of the Winged creature, a father of the Winged creature, a newly hatched father of the Winged creature, and a mother of the Winged creature</li><li>Output: the Winged creature whose mother and father are the input creatures</li><li>Eggs: the combined eggs of the (unhatched) mother and father, minus the eggs of the hatched mother and the hatched father</li></ul>
Bloodthirsty Split	<ul><li>Input: *Five* creatures: a Bloodthirsty creature, a newly hatched mother and a newly hatched father of the Bloodthirsty creature, and some other creature made twice over, once using the newly-hatched mother and once using the newly-hatched father</li><li>Output: The creature input twice over</li><li>Eggs: The combined eggs of the two instances of the output creature in the input bin, plus the eggs of the Bloodthirsty creature in the input bin, minus the eggs of the newly-hatched mother and father</li></ul>

2.8. SOME SAMPLE RECIPES

Bloodthirsty Merge	• Input: any creature • Output: a Bloodthirsty creature having the input creature as either mother or father • Eggs: the eggs of the input creature
Eldritch Split	• Input: an Eldritch creature whose parent is also an Eldritch creature • Output: the Eldritch grandparent of the input creature • Eggs: the eggs of the input creature
Eldritch Merge	• Input: a newly-hatched creature (the parent of the target Eldritch creature), and another creature and its Eldritch offspring • Output: the Eldritch offspring of the first input creature • Eggs: the combined eggs of the creature+Eldritch offspring pair in the input, minus the egg of the newly-hatched parent of the output Eldritch creature

2.8 Some Sample Recipes

"Master Logibeast genetic engineer" is probably a bit strong for someone who's just finished reading the guidebook. You've got all the knowledge now, but it takes time to develop the *skill* of making that Manipulator do what you want it to do. To help you get started, we give three sample recipes here, showing how multiple methods can be brought together to craft more complicated beasts.

1. **Recipe #1: Making a Bloodthirsty Chylziq from scratch**

Eggs	Step	Genetic Method	Input Creatures	Output Creature
(Eldritch Whyndidid)	1	Hatch	-	Eldritch Whyndidid
(Fluftoom)	2	Hatch	-	Fluftoom
(Fluftoom)	3	Bloodthirsty Merge	2	Bloodthirsty Chylziq
(Eldritch Whyndidid)	4	Eldritch Merge	2,3,1	Eldritch Foorghast
(Eldritch Whyndidid)	5	Bloodthirsty Merge	4	Bloodthirsty Chylziq
-	6	Eldritch Merge	1,5,1	Eldritch Rhozoon
-	7	Eldritch Split	6	Bloodthirsty Chylziq

   Or pictorially:

CHAPTER 2. LOGIBEAST GENETIC ENGINEERING

Eggs	Step	Genetic Method	Input Creatures	Output Creature
()	1	Hatch	-	
( )	2	Hatch	-	
( )	3	Bloodthirsty Merge	2	
()	4	Eldritch Merge	2,3,1	
()	5	Bloodthirsty Merge	4	
-	6	Eldritch Merge	1,5,1	
-	7	Eldritch Split	6	

2. **Recipe #2: Making a Primeval Achmemth from scratch**

Eggs	Step	Genetic Method	Input Creatures	Output Creature
(Primeval Gnomoloq)	1	Hatch	-	Primeval Gnomoloq
(Grotesque Ffli)	2	Hatch	-	Grotesque Ffli
(Oolopod)	3	Hatch	-	Oolopod
(Grotesque Ffli)	4	Grotesque Split	2	Ytrrig
(Primeval Gnomoloq, Grotesque Ffli)	5	Primeval Split	1,4	Primeval J'jaklu
(Primeval Gnomoloq, Grotesque Ffli Oolopod)	6	Primeval Split	3,5	Aarobak
(Grotesque Ffli)	7	Grotesque Split	2	Eldritch Webblob
(Primeval Gnomoloq, Grotesque Ffli)	8	Eldritch Merge	3,6,7	Eldritch Iumhfiss
(Primeval Gnomoloq)	9	Primeval Merge	2,8	Primeval Vrilvriktu
-	10	Primeval Merge	1,9	Primeval Achmemth

Or pictorially:

Eggs	Step	Genetic Method	Input Creatures	Output Creature
()	1	Hatch	-	
( )	2	Hatch	-	
( )	3	Hatch	-	
( )	4	Grotesque Split	2	
(,)	5	Primeval Split	1,4	
(, ,)	6	Primeval Split	3,5	
( )	7	Grotesque Split	2	
(,)	8	Eldritch Merge	3,6,7	
()	9	Primeval Merge	2,8	
-	10	Primeval Merge	1,9	

3. **Recipe #3: Making an Oolopod from a Primeval Gtuftbak and a Primeval Inxam**

2.8. SOME SAMPLE RECIPES

Eggs	Step	Genetic Method	Input Creatures	Output Creature
(Primeval Gtuftbak)	1	Hatch	-	Primeval Gtuftbak
(Primeval Inxam)	2	Hatch	-	Primeval Inxam
(Eldritch Iumhfiss)	3	Hatch	-	Eldritch Iumhfiss
(Aarobak)	4	Hatch	-	Aarobak
(Primeval Gtuftbak, Aarobak)	5	Primeval Split	1,4	Oolopod
(Primeval Gtuftbak, Eldritch Iumhfiss)	6	Eldritch Merge	4,3,5	Eldritch Webblob
(Primeval J'jaklu)	7	Hatch	-	Primeval J'jaklu
(Primeval Inxam, Primeval J'jaklu)	8	Primeval Split	2,7	Aarobak
(Primeval Gtuftbak, Primeval Inxam, Eldritch Iumhfiss)	9	Eldritch Merge	7,6,8	Eldritch Effintop
(Oolopod)	10	Hatch	-	Oolopod
(Eldritch Webblob)	11	Hatch	-	Eldritch Webblob
(Eldritch Iumhfiss, Eldritch Webblob)	12	Eldritch Merge	11,10,3	Eldritch Mumfloom
(Eldritch Iumhfiss, Eldritch Webblob)	13	Eldritch Split	12	Aarobak
(Eldritch Iumhfiss)	14	Primeval Merge	10,13	Primeval J'jaklu
(Primeval Gtuftbak, Primeval Inxam)	15	Eldritch Merge	3,9,14	Eldritch Iamimtu
(Primeval Gtuftbak, Primeval Inxam)	16	Eldritch Split	15	Oolopod

Or pictorially:

Eggs	Step	Genetic Method	Input Creatures	Output Creature
(🐾)	1	Hatch	-	🐾
()	2	Hatch	-	
(🍄)	3	Hatch	-	🍄
(🐍)	4	Hatch	-	🐍
(🐾, 🐍)	5	Primeval Split	1,4	
(🐾, 🍄)	6	Eldritch Merge	4,3,5	
()	7	Hatch	-	
(,)	8	Primeval Split	2,7	🐍
(🐾,, 🍄)	9	Eldritch Merge	7,6,8	
(🐑)	10	Hatch	-	🐑
(🐉)	11	Hatch	-	🐉
(🍄, 🐉)	12	Eldritch Merge	11,10,3	
(🍄, 🐉)	13	Eldritch Split	12	🐍
(🍄)	14	Primeval Merge	10,13	
(🐾,)	15	Eldritch Merge	3,9,14	
(🐾,)	16	Eldritch Split	15	🐑

CHAPTER 3

ELEMENTAL ATTACKS AND ELEMENTAL VULNERABILITIES

By now, you've probably got a basement full of genetically engineered Logibeasts. (Remember, damage to the basement, injury to any inhabitants of the house, and profound moral corruption of the surrounding neighborhood are explicitly *not* the legal responsibility of Logibeast™ Corporation. We highly recommend using the included Logizoo 2.0 storage facility once you've accumulated three or more Logibeasts, or even a single Eldritch beast.)

Maybe you're just a fan of xenobiology and are happy simply to visit your Logibeasts each day and learn more about their myriad, and occasionally extraordinarily dangerous, habits. But in all likelihood you, like so many others, have gotten into Logibeast engineering because you want to get involved in (or get a leg (or a tentacle) up on) the world of Logibeast combat.

Being skilled at using the Genetic Manipulator to create a wide range of exotic Logibeasts is crucial for success in Logibeast combat. But you also need a thorough understanding of the ins and outs of the fighting abilities of the beasts. Logibeasts, as you will have noticed by now, come equipped with a wide range of fangs, claws, tentacles, horns, and hats. But despite this rich genetic heritage (yes, including the hats – they are, of course, grown, not bought), when Logibeast fights Logibeast it's not a matter of nature red in tooth and claw. Rather, Logibeast combat is based on beams of *elemental force*.

The first step, then, is to understand Logibeast elemental theory. Logibeasts are animated by, and use in combat, five basic elements:

1. Earth, traditionally represented in the medieval work on the alchemical theory of elements by the symbol ⊗
2. Air, symbolized by ≈
3. Fire, symbolized by 🔥
4. Water, symbolized by 💧
5. Æther, symbolized by ✳

But matched with these five elements are five more "anti-elements":

1. Dark earth, symbolized by ⊗
2. Dark air, synbolized by ≈
3. Dark fire, symbolized by 🔥
4. Dark water, symbolized by 💧
5. Dark Æther, symbolized by ✳

As we'll see soon, there is a close relation between the dark elements and the Eldritch family of Logibeasts.

Each of the basic Logibeasts is associated with a specific element, in the following way:

1. Fluftooms attack with fire
2. Yttrigs attack with æther

3. Aarobaks attack with air

4. Schloofs attack with earth

5. Oolopods attack with water

So, for example, tussling with an annoyed Fluftoom is likely to end up with a fireball or two tossed in your direction. (That's why we always recommend well-insulated gloves when handling Fluftooms. Some recent archaeological work suggests that the Great Fire of London may have been a consequence of early Logibeast breeding experiments by Isaac Newton and Margaret Cavendish.) But if it's your Oolopod you annoy, you'll end up with a flooded, rather than a charred, house.

The Eldritch children of the basic Logibeasts then attack wth the dark versions of their parents' elemental attacks:

1. Eldritch Foorghasts (the Eldritch children of Fluftooms) attack with dark fire.

2. Eldritch M'bimtips (the Eldritch children of Yttrigs) attack with dark æther.

3. Eldritch Webblobs (the Eldritch children of Aarobaks) attack with dark air.

4. Eldritch Izghaams (the Eldritch children of Schloofs) attack with dark earth.

5. Eldritch Iumhfisses (the Eldritch children of Oolopods) attack with dark water.

But with Logibeasts, things never remain simple. To get a full understanding of Logibeast elemental attacks, there are two crucial concepts you need to master: the *stacked attack* and the *pulsed attack*. Let's start with an example of each:

- Consider the Grotesque Gnuffle. When a Grotesque Gnuffle is in an attacking mood, it lets loose with a powerful blast of combined fire and water. (You might have thought fire and water would just cancel each other out in an attack. No such luck – think of it as something like being hit by a tidal wave of boiling water and steam.). Importantly, the fire and water are simultaneous, and bound together into a single attack in which each augments the deadly force of the other.

The combined elemental attack of fire and water is represented using the symbol 🔥💧, with the two elemental symbols for fire and water bound in a single oval to mark their combined stacked nature.

We'll talk more about the *vulnerabilities* of Logibeasts to elemental attacks in a bit, but looking ahead briefly: one of the things that's characteristic of a *stacked* attack is that it's powerful enough to defeat a beast that's vulnerable to either component of the attack. So a beast that's vulnerable to fire will be defeated by the elemental attack of the Grotesque Gnuffle, because of the fire component of the combined attack. And a beast that's vulnerable to water will also be defeated by the elemental attack of the Grotesque Gnuffle, because of the water component of the combined attack.

(Logibeast cogniscenti among the readers may have noticed that the Grotesque Gnuffle, with its combined fire+water attack, is the Grotesque offspring of a Fluftoom, with its attack of fire, and an Oolopod, with its attack of water. That's no coincidence. We'll say more about this soon when we talk about using genealogy to determine Logibeast attack modes.)

- Consider the Bloodthirsty Cavaidko. An angry Cavaidko launches an attack that combines earth and water. But it's not a *combined* attack of earth and water. Instead, it's a *pulsed* attack. That means that the attack rapidly alternates between an earth-based attack and a water-based attack. Now, that's not to say that you won't get rather muddy should you have the bad luck to confront an enraged Bloodthirsty Cavaidko. But that's a minor side effect, rather than the centerpiece of the attack. You'll never at any one moment be under assault both through the element of water and through the element of earth.

A pulsed attack of earth and water is represented using the symbol (🌐) + (💧), where the + symbol indicates the pulsing alternation of the two elemental forms.

Again, more on vulnerabilities soon, but the key point is that a beast won't be defeated by a pulsed attack unless it's vulnerable to *both* aspects of the alternating pulses. If a creature is vulnerable to earth but not water, then it can withstand the attack of a Bloodthirsty Cavaidko. The hurling boulders of the earthy moments of the Cavaidko's attack do their damage, but while the water component of the attack is (literally!) washing over the creature with no damaging effects, it's able to recover sufficiently to withstand the next pulse of earth. Similarly, if a creature is vulnerable to water but not earth, it can also withstand the attack of a Bloodthirsty Cavaidko. In this case, it takes intermittent earth breathers to recover from the water component of the attack. *But* if a Bloodthirsty Cavaidko has the good luck to confront a creature vulnerable to *both* earth *and* water, the Cavaidko can emerge triumphant. Both parts of the pulsing attack hit vulnerabilities of the target creature, and it falls under the overall pulsed attack.

(More foreshadowing for the cogniscenti: it's not an accident that the Bloodthirsty Cavaidko is the Bloodthirsty offspring of a Schloof, with its elemental attack of earth, and an Oolopod, with its elemental attack of water.)

If your goal is to design Logibeasts for combat, you won't get far just genetically engineering beasts at random and then just throwing them into the arena to see what their elemental attacks are. You need to understand the *theory* of Logibeast attacks so that you can work out in advance how your carefully crafted creature will lash out against its opponent. The key idea behind Logibeast attacks is this:

> **Genealogy Determines Elementology**: To work out how a given Logibeast will attack, you need to think through the family tree of that beast.

The key idea is simple enough, but the details get to be a bit convoluted. But have no fear: a little practice and you'll soon be as adept in fighting Logibeasts as you already are at creating them.

3.1 The Bloodthirsty Rule

Because genealogy determines elementology, if you want to know how a given Logibeast attacks, the first step is to look at the family tree of that beast. Let's start with an easy one. Consider the

60 CHAPTER 3. ATTACKS AND VULNERABILITIES

Bloodthirsty Awtroof. Consulting the Logibestiary, here is the family tree of the Awtroof:

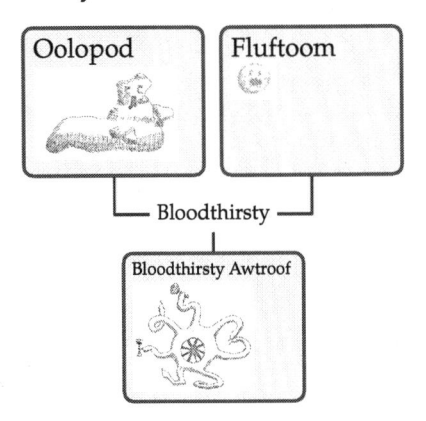

We already know that Oolopods attack with water and Fluftooms attack with fire, so we can add this information to the family tree:

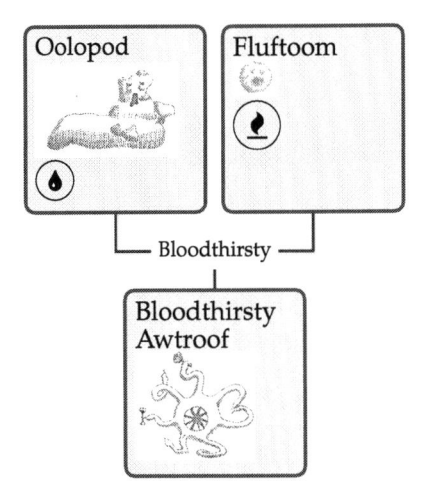

We then introduce the first genealogical rule:

> **The Bloodthirsty Rule**: Bloodthirsty creatures always attack using a pulsing combination of their two parents' attack modes.

The Bloodthirsty Awtroof has as its parents an Oolopod attacking with water and a Fluftoom attacking with fire, so the Bloodthirsty Awtroof attacks with a pulsed combination of fire and water:

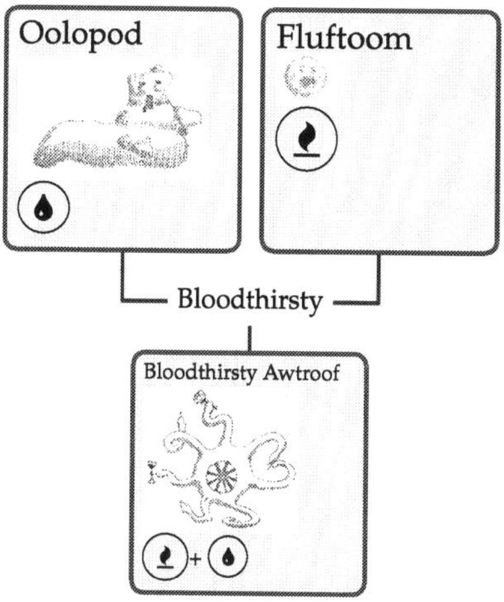

Or suppose you're curious about how your Bloodthirsty Chylziq will do in a fight. Consulting the ever-handy Logibestiary, we put together a family tree for the Bloodthirsty Chylziq:

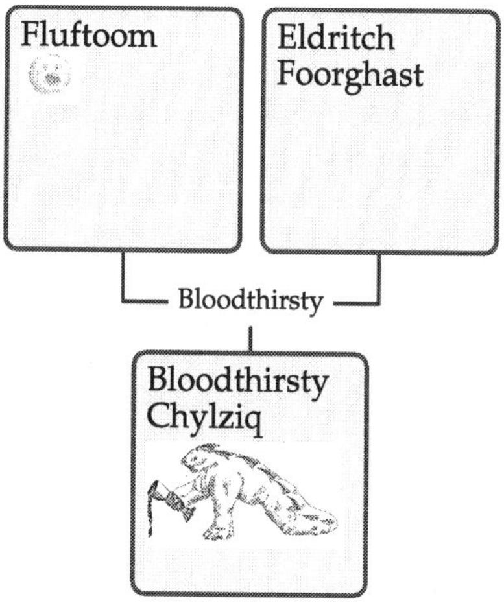

Fluftooms, of course, are fire attackers. Eldritch Foorghasts, being the Eldritch children of Fluftooms, attack with dark fire. Let's add that information to the tree:

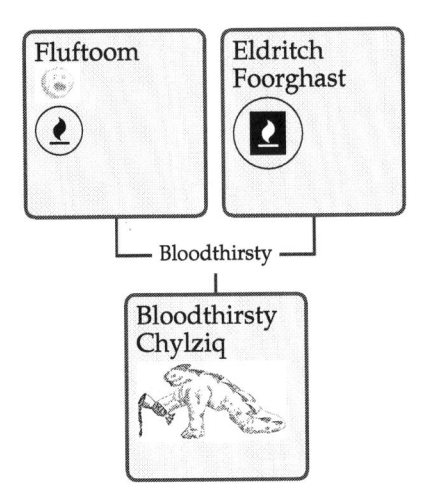

[Fluftoom] [Eldritch Foorghast]
— Bloodthirsty —
[Bloodthirsty Chylziq]

Time again for the Bloodthirsty Rule. Since the Bloodthirsty Chylziq is the Bloodthirsty offspring of a Fluftoom and an Eldritch Foorghast, its attack pulses the attacks of its two parents. So you can expect from your Bloodthirsty Chylziq alternating pulses of fire and dark fire. (We'll see in a bit that this makes the Bloodthirsty Chylziq a bit of a lightweight in the combat arena. Bad for your Logibeast win count, but it does make the Bloodthirsty Chylziq an excellent children's pet. If they don't mind the smell. And the sound.) That gives us the full tree:

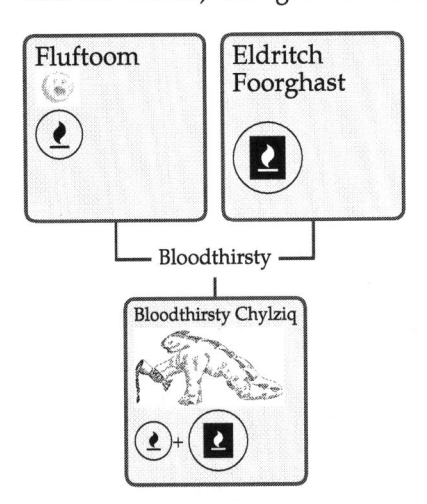

[Fluftoom] [Eldritch Foorghast]
— Bloodthirsty —
[Bloodthirsty Chylziq]

Ah, but what if your Bloodthirsty creature doesn't have two parents that are both basic beasts? No problem; the Bloodthirsty Rule

3.1. THE BLOODTHIRSTY RULE

still applies. What, for example, should you expect from your Bloodthirsty Azill? Consulting the Logibestiary, here's the family tree for the Bloodthirsty Azill:

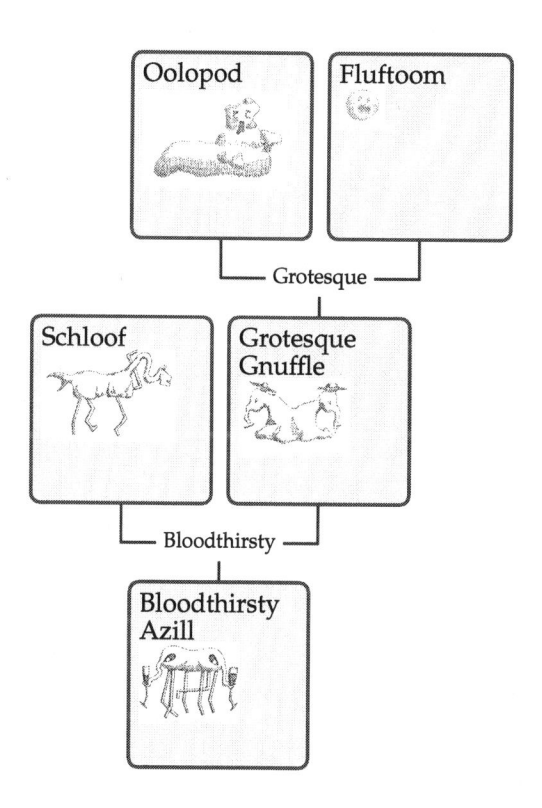

By now you should recognize the elemental attacks of the basic Logibeasts, so go ahead and fill in the attacks of the Oolopod, the Fluftoom, and the Schloof. And we mentioned earlier that the Grotesque Gnuffle inherits from its parents a combine fire+water attack. That gives us:

64 CHAPTER 3. ATTACKS AND VULNERABILITIES

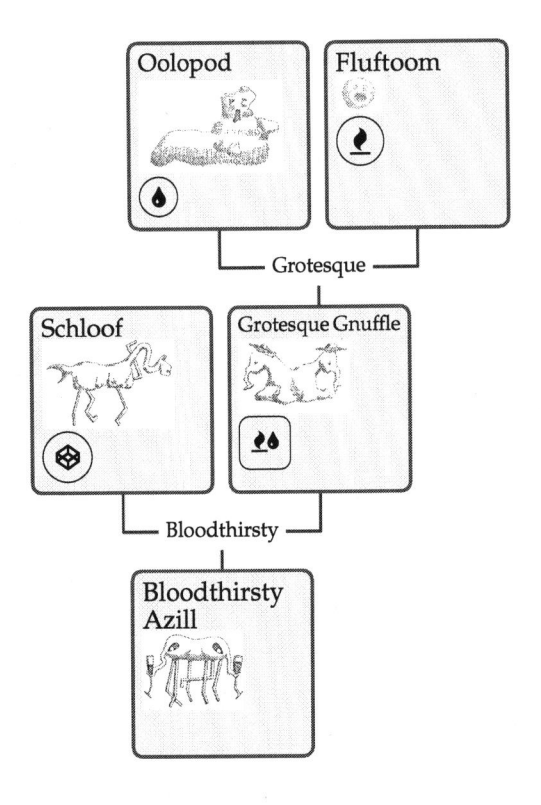

```
┌──────────┐  ┌──────────┐
│ Oolopod  │  │ Fluftoom │
│          │  │          │
│   (💧)   │  │   (🔥)   │
└────┬─────┘  └─────┬────┘
     └── Grotesque ──┘
          │
┌──────────┐  ┌──────────────────┐
│ Schloof  │  │ Grotesque Gnuffle│
│          │  │                  │
│   (🜨)   │  │     (🔥💧)       │
└────┬─────┘  └─────┬────────────┘
     └── Bloodthirsty ──┘
          │
     ┌──────────┐
     │Bloodthirsty│
     │   Azill    │
     │            │
     └────────────┘
```

And now, just apply the Bloodthirsty Rule. Nothing to it! The parents of the Bloodthirsty Azill attack with earth (the Schloof) and a fire+water combination (the Grotesque Gnuffle), so the Bloodthirsty Azill just alternates these two attacks for its pulsing attack:

3.1. THE BLOODTHIRSTY RULE

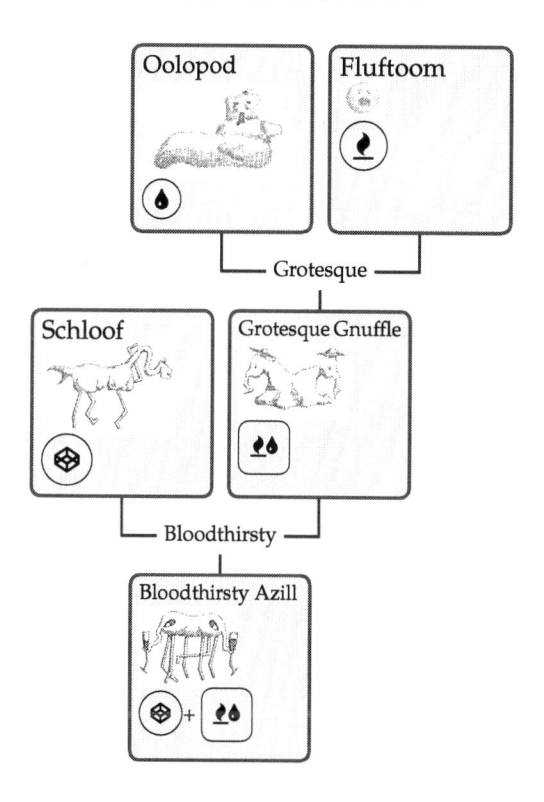

Your Bloodthirsty Azill, then, is going to give you alternating bursts of earth and of a fire-and-water combination.

OK, let's look at one more example of the Bloodthirsty Rule. What kind of violence is a Bloodthirsty Blijjif going to deal out in combat? As usual, start with the family tree of the Blijjjif:

66   CHAPTER 3. ATTACKS AND VULNERABILITIES

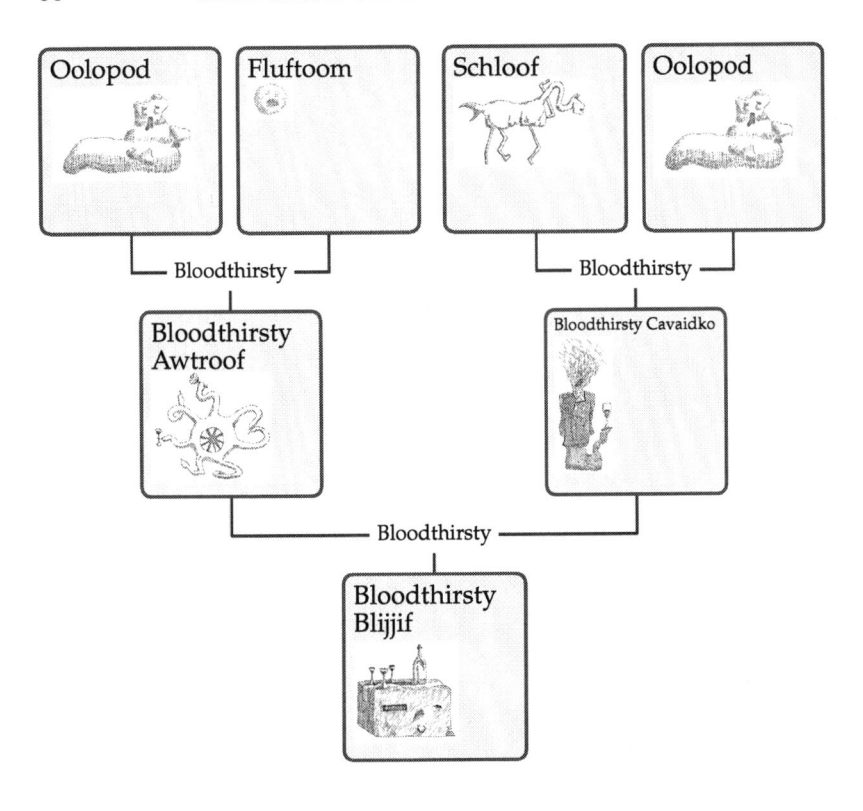

```
  Oolopod      Fluftoom       Schloof        Oolopod
     |             |              |              |
     +—Bloodthirsty—+             +—Bloodthirsty—+
              |                           |
       Bloodthirsty              Bloodthirsty Cavaidko
         Awtroof
              |                           |
              +———————Bloodthirsty————————+
                           |
                     Bloodthirsty
                        Blijjif
```

Stick in the attacks of the basic beasts, and apply the Bloodthirsty Rule twice, once for the Bloodthirsty Awtroof and once for the Bloodthirsty Cavaidko:

3.1. THE BLOODTHIRSTY RULE

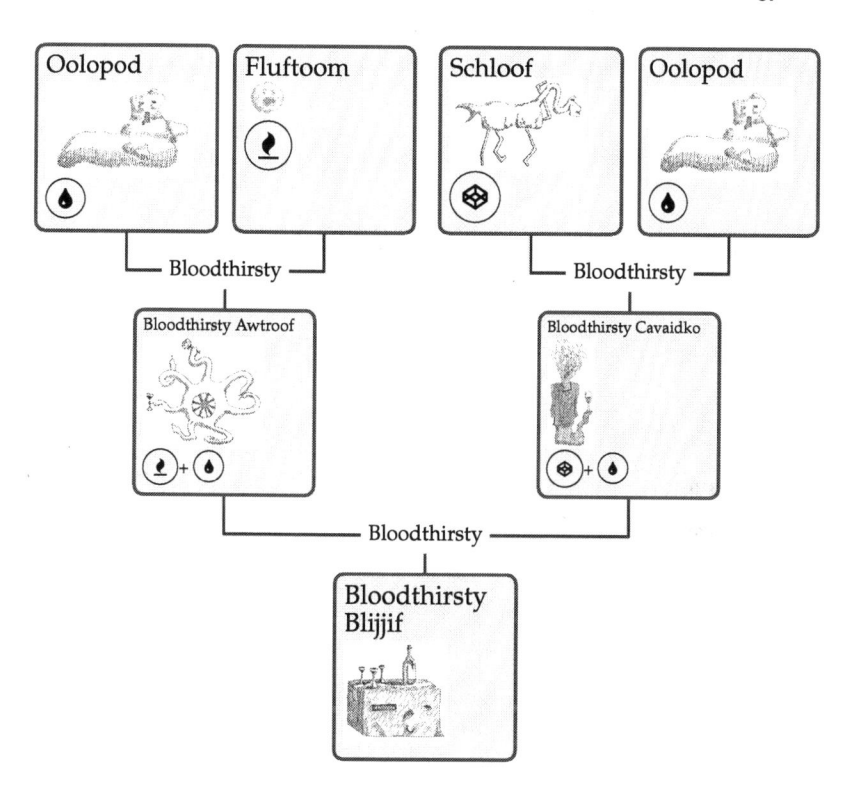

What about the Bloodthirsty Blijjif? Well, just apply the Bloodthirsty Rule again. The Blijjif is going to pulse the attacks of its two parents, so it is going to alternate a fire-alternating-with-water attack with a earth-alternating-with-water attack. That's easy to symbolize – just put a plus between the two attacks to make (🔥)+(💧)+(🟦)+(💧):

CHAPTER 3. ATTACKS AND VULNERABILITIES

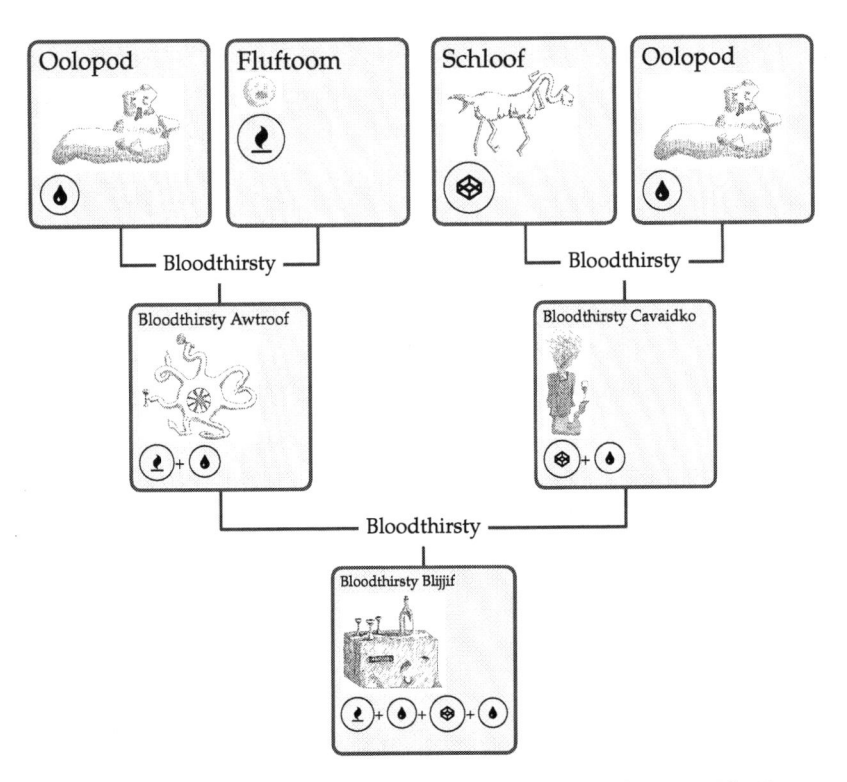

And there you have it: the attack form of the Bloodthirsty Blijjif. You should learn from the example of the Bloodthirsty Blijjif that a Logibeast can have a pulsing attack with more than one alternating component. In fact, there's no upper limit on the number of alternating elemental forms that can make up a Logibeast's attack. There can be a beast that alternates all of the five basic elemental forms:

- ⊛ + ≈ + ♨ + ◉ + ✹

Or even all of the elements *and* all of the dark elements:

- ⊛ + ≈ + ♨ + ◉ + ✹ + ⊛ + ≈ + ♨ + ◉ + ✹

And there can be beasts that pulse long sequences of combined elemental attacks, such as:

3.1. THE BLOODTHIRSTY RULE

- (earth≈air✹) + (≈air💧water) + (💧fire🔥) + (💧≈water☀)

That's a beast whose pulsed attack first sends a combination of earth, air, and ether; and then sends a combination of air, fire, and water; and then sends a combination of fire, water, and dark fire; and finally sends a combination of water, dark air, dark water, and dark ether. Fun challenge once you've gone through the basics of this tutorial on Logibeast attacks: pull out your Genetic Manipulator and see if you can create a beast that has that attack form.

> **A Note for The Impatient**: There is, admittedly, something a bit odd about the attack form we've determined for the Bloodthirsty Blijjif. Alternating fire, water, earth, and water? That seems a bit redundant. Seems? Nay, it is. It turns out to be a *harmless* redundancy, but it is indeed redundant. No need to mention *twice* that water is among the elements that the Bloodthirsty Blijjif pulses. It would do just as well to call the Blijjif attack (fire) + (water) + (earth).

That's an instance of a general rule of simplification:

> **Simplification**: If an elemental attack mode is mentioned more than once in the pulsing sequence for a Logibeast, the repeated mentions can be harmlessly dropped. For those who like fancy formulations, that's to say that an attack of the form:
>
> - $\ldots + (X) + \ldots + (X) + \ldots$
>
> is the same thing as an attack of the form:
>
> - $\ldots + (X) + \ldots$
>
> where one of the two mentions of (X) has been omitted.

Simplification saves you some time in recording Logibeast attacks in your notes, and sometimes makes it easier to see what's going on. But the nice thing about Simplification is that it's also completely optional. You won't go wrong if you leave Logibeast attack descriptions unsimplified – you'll get the same correct predictions for all Logibeast combats. So simplify only if you want to and you find it helpful.

Final note: if you *do* simply, do it right. We recommend making sure you can pass the following quick diagnostic quiz before doing any simplification of your own.

1. **First Question**: Does $\boxed{💧💧} + \boxed{💧} + \boxed{💧} + \boxed{💧💧}\boxed{💧}$ simplify to $\boxed{💧💧} + \boxed{💧} + \boxed{💧}$?

   - **Answer: Yes.** $\boxed{💧💧} + \boxed{💧} + \boxed{💧} + \boxed{💧💧}\boxed{💧}$ contains two occurrences of $\boxed{💧}$, so we can get rid of one of them. And it also contains two occurrences of $\boxed{💧💧}$, so we can get rid of one of them.

2. **Second Question**: Does $\boxed{≈💧💧} + \boxed{💧💧}$ simplify to $\boxed{≈} + \boxed{💧💧}$?

   - **Answer: No.** It's true that both $\boxed{💧}$ and $\boxed{💧}$ *occur in* both of the two components of the pulsed attack $\boxed{≈💧💧} + \boxed{💧💧}$. But neither $\boxed{💧}$ nor $\boxed{💧}$ by themselves *is* one of the components of the pulsed attack, so neither one can be deleted. $\boxed{≈💧💧} + \boxed{💧💧}$ doesn't simplify.

3. **Third Question**: Does $\boxed{≈} + \boxed{✦} + \boxed{≋} + \boxed{💧💧}$ simply to $\boxed{≈} + \boxed{✦} + \boxed{💧💧}$?

   - **Answer: No.** The attack $\boxed{≈} + \boxed{✦} + \boxed{≋} + \boxed{💧💧}$ does contain both an air and a dark air component. But that doesn't count as a redundacy. Air and dark air are different elemental modes, so we don't want to drop the mention of either one of them. ((≈)+(✵)+(≈)+[💧], on the other hand, would simplify to (≈)+(✵)+[💧], because it mentions (≈) twice, unnecessarily.)

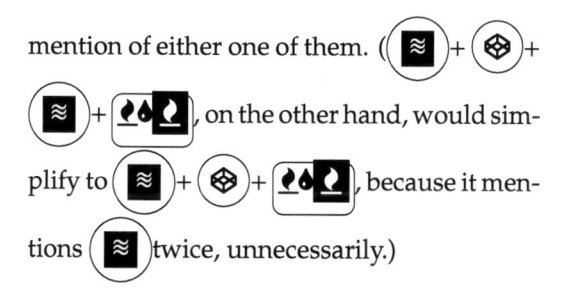

3.2 The Grotesque Rule

OK, so much for the Bloodthirsty Rule. But, as they say, as with the Bloodthirsty, so with the Grotesque. So next we'll learn about the Grotesque Rule. Here it is:

> **The Grotesque Rule**: Grotesque creatures always attack using a stacked combination of their two parents' attack modes.

The basic idea is simple, but as we'll see, in certain cases the Grotesque Rule introduces some complications we didn't have to deal with in the case of the Bloodthirsty Rule. Let's start easy, though. Consider the Grotesque Ogrit. Here's its family tree:

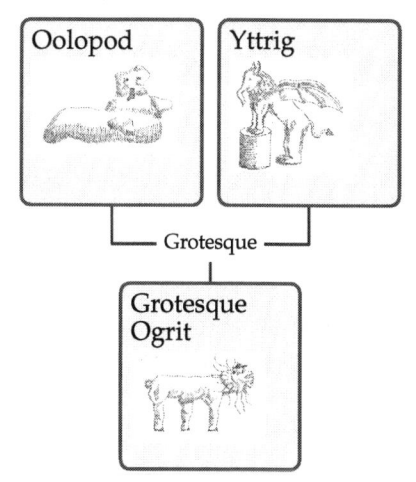

Oolopod | Yttrig
— Grotesque —
Grotesque Ogrit

Oolopods attack with water and Yttrigs attack with æther, so by the Grotesque Rule, Grotesque Ogrits attack with a stacked combination of water and æther. Thus:

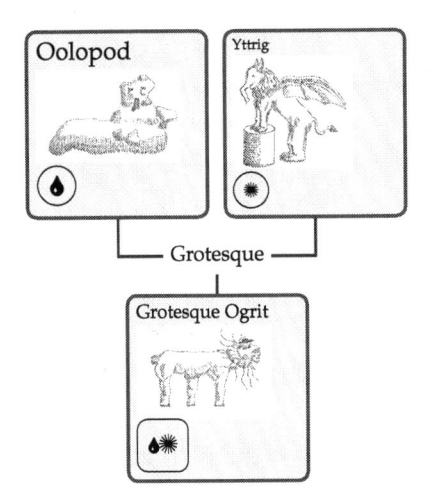

[Oolopod] [Yttrig]
— Grotesque —
[Grotesque Ogrit]

Or consider the Grotesque Ffli. Here's its family tree, with all the powers indicated:

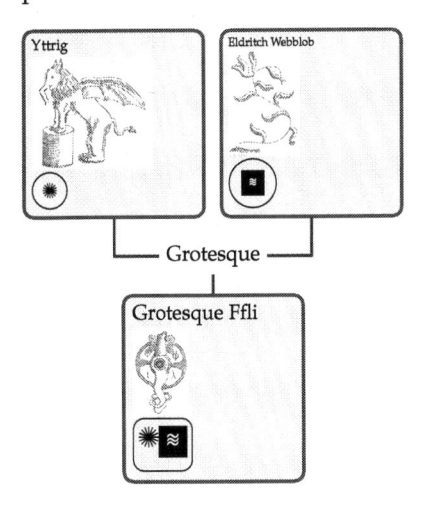

[Yttrig] [Eldritch Webblob]
— Grotesque —
[Grotesque Ffli]

A Yttrig attacks with æther and an Eldritch Webblob attacks with dark air, so their Grotesque offspring the Grotesque Ffli attacks with a stacked combination of æther and dark air, as the Grotesque Rule indicates.

For a slightly more complicated case, consider the Grotesque Ushtrimbot. The Grotesque Ushtrimbot is the Grotesque offspring of a Grotesque Gnuffle and a Grotesque Ffli, so its full family tree is:

3.2. THE GROTESQUE RULE

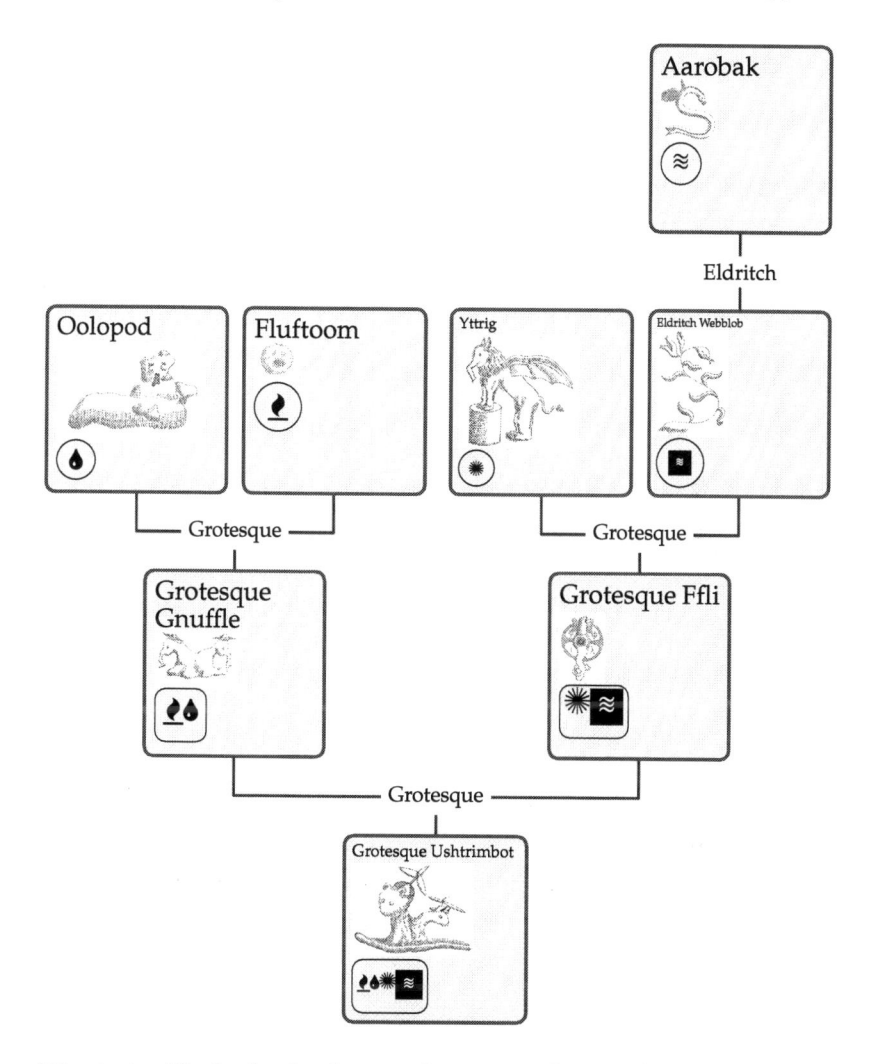

[Diagram: Creature family tree]

- **Aarobak** (air) — Eldritch → **Eldritch Webblob** (dark air)
- **Oolopod** (water) + **Fluftoom** (fire) — Grotesque → **Grotesque Gnuffle** (fire + water)
- **Yttrig** (æther) + **Eldritch Webblob** (dark air) — Grotesque → **Grotesque Ffli** (æther + dark air)
- **Grotesque Gnuffle** + **Grotesque Ffli** — Grotesque → **Grotesque Ushtrimbot**

We start with the basic elemental powers of water for the Oolopod, fire for the Fluftoom, æther for the Yttrig, and air for the Aarobak. We already know that the Eldritch Webblob, being the Eldritch offspring of the air-using Aarobak, fights with dark air. (We'll learn more generally about combat abilities of Eldritch creatures soon.) We then use the Grotesque rule twice to learn (again!) that the Grotesque Grotesque Gnuffle fights with fire stacked with air, or [fire+air], and the Grotesque Ffli fights with æther stacked with dark air, or [æther+dark air]. So to get the combat ability of the Grotesque

Ushtrimbot, we just use the Grotesque Rule one more time, stack everything together, and get [💧☀≈]. The Grotesque Ushtrimbot attacks with a formidable stacked combination of fire, water, æther, and dark air. (If you've engineered an Ushtrimbot, we do highly recommend you stay on its good side. The occasional mackerel as a treat is surprisingly effective in restoring the good humor of an Ushtrimbot.)

"Stack everything together" sounds like a nice easy rule, but unfortunately things aren't always quite so simple. Consider the case of the Grotesque Oivuut. Here is the family tree of the Oivuut:

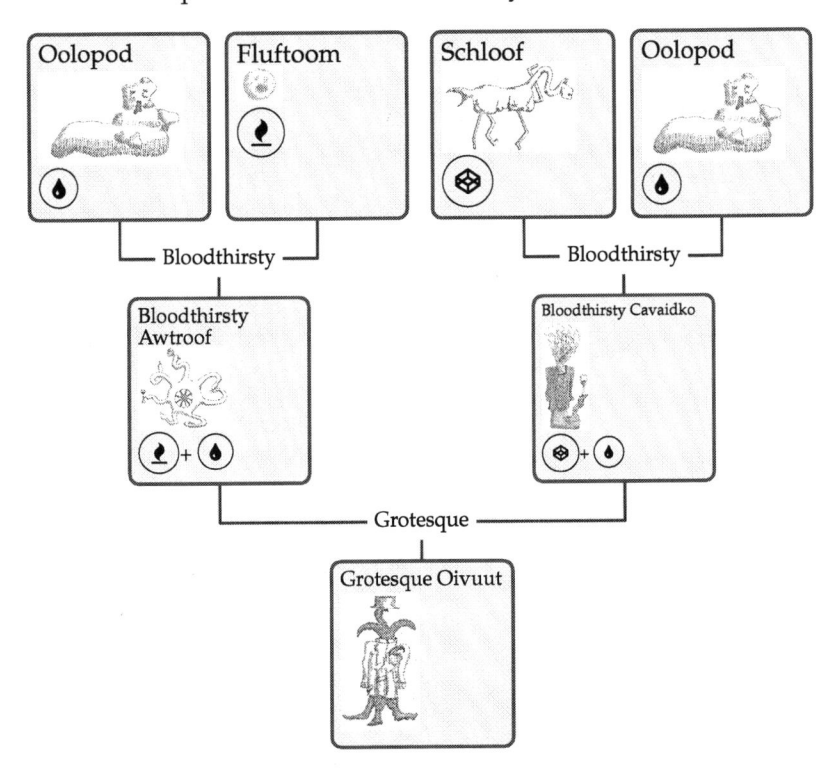

The two parents of the Grotesque Oivutt are the Bloodthirsty Awtroof, which attacks with a pulsing fire and water combination, and the Bloodthirsty Cavaidko, which attacks with a pulsing earth and water combination. The Grotesque Rule tells us that the Grotesque Oivutt should attack with a stacked combination of its parents' attacks. But how do you stack two *pulsed* attacks?

3.2. THE GROTESQUE RULE

To answer this, it's time for you to learn one of the things that sets apart the truly expert Logibeast combatants: the **Box Method**.

> **The Box Method**: To stack two pulsed attacks, make a rectangular grid with the pulsed components of one pulsed attack along the horizontal length of the rectangle and the pulsed components of the other pulsed attack along the vertical width of the rectangle. So, to stack the (🔥)+(💧) attack of the Bloodthirsty Awtroof with the (🧊)+(💧) attack of the Bloodthirsty Cavaidko, we start with the rectangle like this:

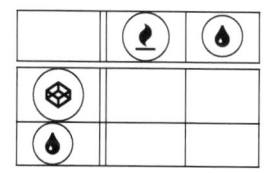

	🔥	💧
🧊		
💧		

(In this particular case, the rectangle is actually a square, but that won't always be the case.) We've put the Bloodthirsty Awtroof's attacks on the horizontal and the Bloodthirsty Cavaidko's attacks on the vertical.

Now, *stack* attacks within each cell of the grid. For example, the upper left (empty) cell is on the (🧊) row and the (🔥) column, so in it, we put a stacked earth-and-fire attack. Filling in the rest of the grid, we get:

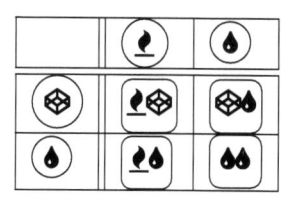

	🔥	💧
🧊	🔥🧊	🧊💧
💧	🔥💧	💧💧

Finally, make a *pulsed* attack out of the four cells of the grid to produce the final attack. So the Grotesque Oivutt's attack mode is $\boxed{🔥🧊} + \boxed{🧊💧} + \boxed{🔥💧} + \boxed{💧💧}$. It's a pulsed attack in which the four pulses are (i) a stacked combination of fire and earth, (ii) a stacked combination of earth and water, (iii) a stacked combination of fire and earth, and (iv) a stacked combination of water and water. (Of course, using Simplification, we could just say water for that last pulse, rather than water-stacked-with-water.)

So, for your viewing pleasure, here's the complete family tree of the Grotesque Oivutt, with all attack modes included:

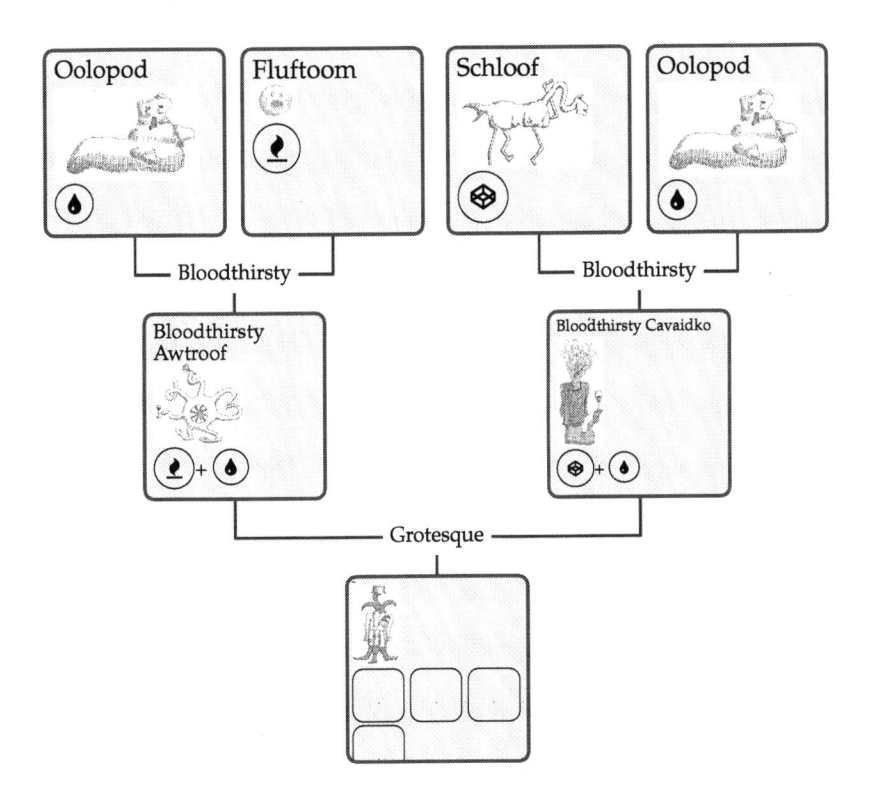

The Box Method makes it easy to apply the Grotesque Rule, but it does take a while to get completely used to using the method. Let's go through one more example. Consider the charming Grotesque Tvunglit. Here is its family tree, with the attacks of all of its ancestors included.

3.2. THE GROTESQUE RULE

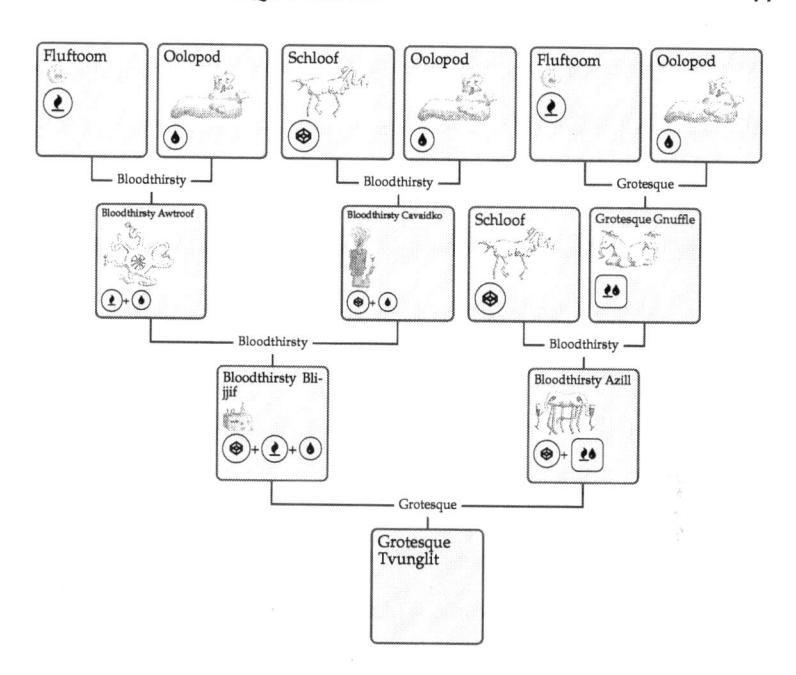

What about the Grotesque Tvunglit itself? Well, we need to apply the Grotesque Rule, which means it's time for the Box Method again. We'll put the pulsed attacks of the Bloodthirsty Blijjif on the horizontal and the pulsed attacks of the Bloodthirsty Azill on the vertical. That gives us this grid:

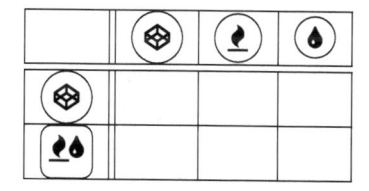

Next, fill in the grid using the Grotesque Rule to stack elements:

Combining everything into a pulsed attack and doing some Simplifying, we've got it. The attack of the Grotesque Tvunglit is

⬣ + ⬣⋆ + ⬣● + ⬣⋆● + ⋆●.

So that's it for Grotesque creatures. By using the Box Method to apply the Grotesque Rule, you can work out the powers of any Grotesque creature you're able to construct, as long as you know the attack modes of its parents.

3.3 The Eldritch Rule

On then to Eldritch creatures. As we've already mentioned, Eldritch creatures have a fundamental affinity to the dark elements. But that doesn't mean that every Eldritch creature attacks with dark elements. We've already mentioned that the Eldritch Webblob attacks with dark air, since the Eldritch Webblob is the Eldritch offspring of the Aarobak, which attacks with air. But what about the Eldritch Mumfloom, which is the Eldritch offspring of the Eldritch Webblob? The Webblob is *already* attacking with a dark element, so what's left for the Eldritch Mumfloom? Is it supposed to attack with *really* dark air?

Well, yes, kind of. But to know what that means, you have to understand a bit more about the dark elements. The Eldritch Mumfloom attacks with *dark* dark air. But dark dark air isn't air that's even darker than dark air. Remember, the dark elements are *anti-elements*. When you darken dark air, you take a kind of opposite of dark air, which brings you right back to air where you started. (OK, technically: when you *darken* an element you're actually running it through a Möbius transform loop in an involuted non-Hausdorff semi-temporal dimension. Do it twice and quasi-phase gets rotated back to its starting position. But we're guessing you don't really want the gory details.)

So here is the attack-annotated family tree of the Eldritch Mumfloom:

3.3. THE ELDRITCH RULE

[Aarobak] → Eldritch → [Eldritch Webblob] → Eldritch → [Eldritch Mumfloom]

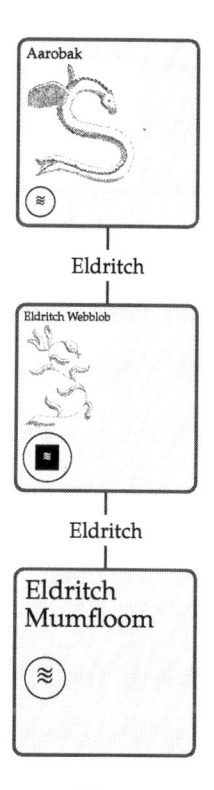

The Eldritch Mumfloom, then, is right back where its grandparent is, attacking with air. It's the old story: rebel against your parents, end up just like your grandparents. (Speculation that this pattern is evidence of a trace of the Eldritch in the human genome has never gotten beyond the crackpot level.)

The Eldritch Mumfloom and the Aarobak have the same elemental attack. As we'll see in a bit, that means in combat they'll have a destructive tie, with each destroying the other. And here's a little foreshadowing of a bit of high Logigenetic theory: from an Aarobak egg you can engineer an Eldritch Mumloom, and from an Eldritch Mumfloom egg you can engineer an Aarobak. The second of these is pretty obvious, as the following recipe shows:

Eggs	Step	Genetic Method	Input Creatures	Output Creature
(Eldritch Mumfloom)	1	Hatch	-	Eldritch Mumloom
(Eldritch Mumfloom)	2	Eldritch Split	1	Aarobak

The first is slightly less obvious, but still not too hard for the experienced geneticist to whip up:

CHAPTER 3. ATTACKS AND VULNERABILITIES

Eggs	Step	Genetic Method	Input Creatures	Output Creature
(Aarobak)	1	Hatch	-	Aarobak
(Eldritch Webblob)	2	Hatch	-	Eldritch Webblob
(Aarobak)	3	Eldritch Merge 2,1,2	Eldritch Mumfloom	

More about this at the end of this guide, when we have a brief overview of Grand Unified Logibeast Theory for those who are interested in exploring the theoretical side of Logibeast engineering. But you can't become a theorist until after you've mastered the practicalities, and you definitely aren't done with all the practicalities yet. For example, there's a lot more to say about the attacks of Eldritch creatures.

Consider the Eldritch F'nafkor, the Eldritch offspring of the Grotesque Ffli. We've already seen that the attack of the Grotesque Ffli is ※≈. So you might have expected that we could just *darken* each of these individual elements, making æther into dark æther and dark air into air, and get an attack of ※≈ for the Eldritch F'nafkor. But no, the Eldritch creatures never make things that easy for us. The tendency of Eldritch creatures to invert everything goes beyond changing elements into their anti-elements. It also changes stacked attacks into pulsed attacks. So, in fact, the attack of the Eldritch F'nafkor is (※)+(≈).

Eldritch creatures change stacked attacks into pulsed attacks, but they also change pulsed attacks into stacked attacks. So consider the Eldritch Whyndidid. It's the Eldritch offspring of the Bloodthirsty Chylziq. The Chylziq's attack is the pulsed attack (♦)+(♦). The Eldritch effect then changes fire into dark fire, and dark fire into fire. But it also changes the *pulsed* attack into a *stacked* attack. So the Eldritch Whyndidid attacks with ♦♦. As we'll see later, this makes the Eldritch Whyndidid a formidable opponent indeed.

So, elements to their anti-elements, stacked attacks to pulsed attacks, pulsed attacks to stacked attacks. That's the Eldritch way:

> **The Eldritch Rule**: Eldritch creatures always attack with an "inverted" version of their parent's attack, which changes elements to their anti-elements, stacked

3.3. THE ELDRITCH RULE

attacks to pulsed attacks, and pulsed attacks to stacked attacks.

But there are details still to be worked out in complicated cases. Consider the Eldritch Dkbaino. Here is its family tree, complete with the attacks of all of its ancestors:

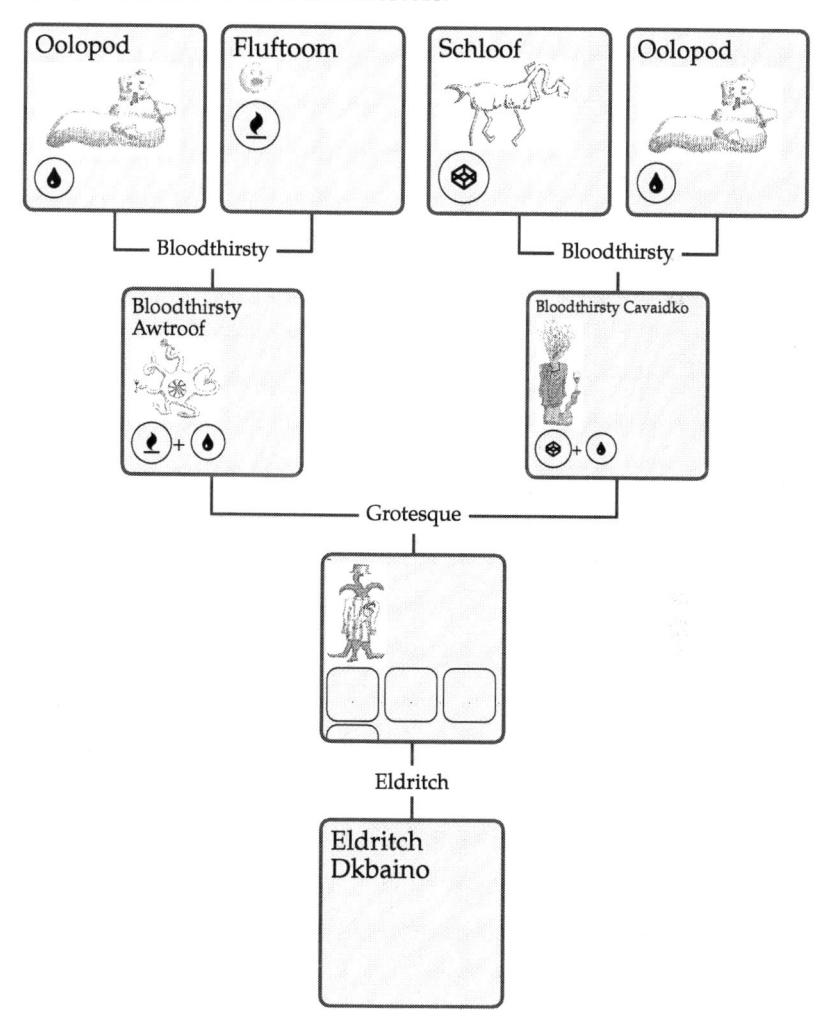

We need to apply the Eldritch Rule to the Grotesque Oivuut's attack of ⬚ + ⬚ + ⬚ + ⬚. Changing the elements to their anti-elements is easy enough:

- ⬚+⬚+⬚+⬚.

But if we change stacked attacks to pulsed attacks and pulsed attacks to stacked attacks, we then get:

- A stacked attack that stacks (i) a pulsed attack of dark fire and dark earth, (ii) a pulsed attack of dark earth and dark water, (iii) a pulsed attack of dark fire and dark water, and (iv) an attack of dark water.

But that's gibberish – you can't stack pulsed attacks. (It's so thoroughly gibberish that we had to use a gibberish-friendly language like English to say it, rather than writing it out using our alchemical representation symbols for attacks.)

Fortunately, this is a problem you've already encountered – and solved. The Grotesque Rule tells us to stack attacks of the parent creatures, and those attacks might be pulsed attacks. So the Grotesque Rule can tell us to stack pulsed attacks. Gibberish again! The Box Method is the way around the gibberish. To "stack" the pulsed attacks (≈)+(✹) and (🔥)+(💧), we use the Box Method:

So the "stacking" of those two pulsed attacks creates the pulsed attack ≈🔥 + ≈💧 + ✹🔥 + ✹💧, with its four stacked components.

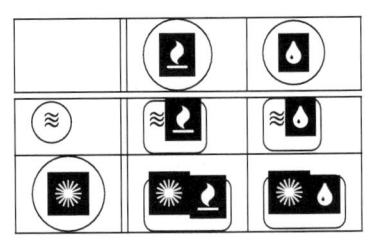

That's our solution to the problem of the Eldritch Dkbaino, then. We take the four components of the Grotesque Oivutt's pulsed attack, invert their elements, and convert each of those components into a pulsed attack. That gives us:

- (🔥)+(⬚)

3.3. THE ELDRITCH RULE

- (⊛) + (💧)
- (🕯) + (💧)
- (💧)

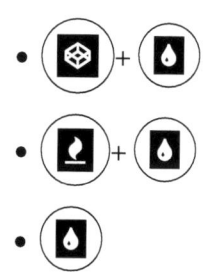

And now we want to use the Box Method on those four pulsed attacks.

But wait! How do we use the Box Method on *four* pulsed attacks. One on the horinzontal length of the rectangle and one on the vertical width of the rectangle, but what about the other two? Fieldwork suggests that the Eldritch beasts themselves use *four dimensional boxes* to calculate Eldritch attacks, but we recommend against this unless you've got some impressive four-dimensional visualization skills up your sleeve. (Are sleeves where one keeps four-dimensional visualization skills?) Fortunately, there is an easier method.

When there are more than two pulsed attacks that need to be combined, we can just use the Box Method multiple times. For the Eldritch Dkbaino, we can first use the Box Method on the two pulsed attacks (🕯) + (⊛) and (⊛) + (💧):

	🕯	⊛
⊛	⊛🕯	⊛
💧	🕯💧	⊛💧

That gives us the pulsed attack ⊛🕯 + ⊛ + 🕯💧 + ⊛💧.

We used to have four different pulsed attacks to stack, but having stacked the first two, we're down to three to stack:

- ⊛🕯 + ⊛ + 🕯💧 + ⊛💧.

CHAPTER 3. ATTACKS AND VULNERABILITIES

- ⬡ + ⬡

- ⬡

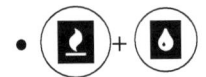

Time to use the Box Method again, now on the two pulsed attacks

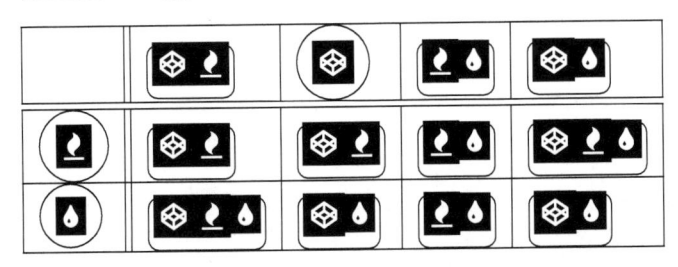

⬡ + ⬡ + ⬡ + ⬡ and ⬡ + ⬡.

[box method table]

That gives us ⬡ + ⬡ + ⬡ + ⬡. (We're applying the Rule of Simplification silently in the background to keep things manageable.) So now there are only two attacks left to stack:

- ⬡ + ⬡ + ⬡ + ⬡

- ⬡

Only more more application of the Box Method left (and a really easy one at that):

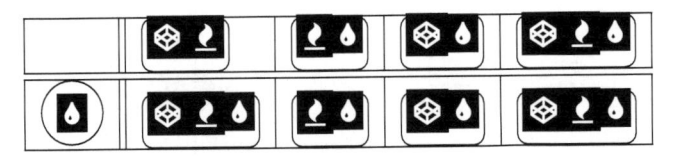

[box method table]

And there we have it: the final attack form of the Eldritch Dkbaino is ⬡ + ⬡ + ⬡. We can now complete the family tree:

3.3. THE ELDRITCH RULE

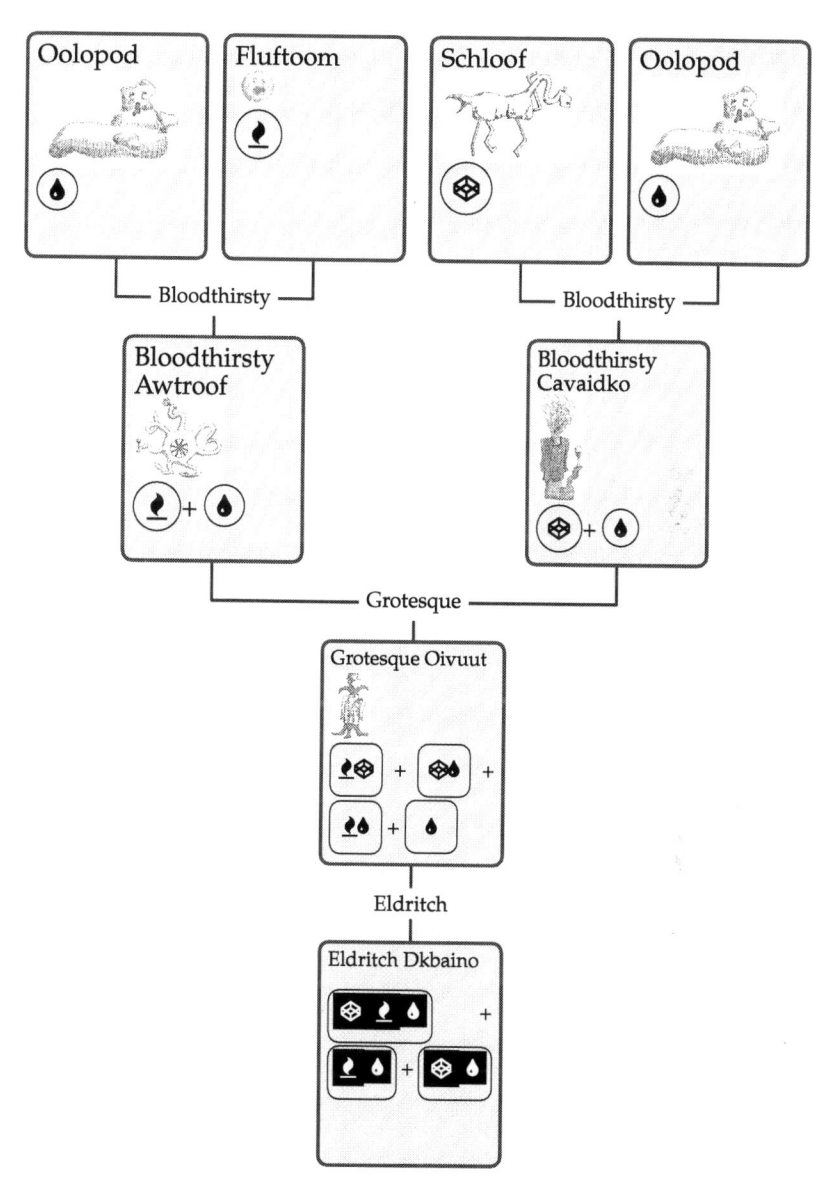

As usual, those Eldritch creatures are a nuisance to deal with. Let's run through the procedure once more:

1. Start with the attack mode of the parent of the Eldritch creature.

2. Go through that attack and invert each elemental component

of it.

3. Take each stacked component of the overall pulsed attack and convert it into an individual pulsed attack.

4. Then take all of the resulting pulsed attacks and combine them two at a time using the Box Method.

It can be slow going, but that will get you through the attack abilities of any Eldritch beast.

3.4 The Primeval Rule

We're past the worst of it now. You still need to be able to calculate the attack abilities of Primeval and Winged beasts, but there aren't any new *ideas* needed for either of these. (Although the actual calculations, especially for the Winged beasts, can be lengthy and annoying.) Let's start with the Primeval beasts.

Consider the Primeval Schniftoo:

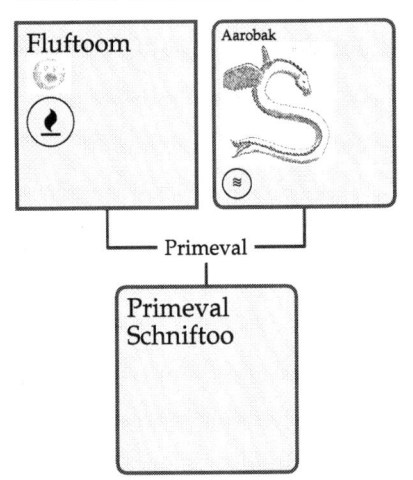

To get the attack mode of a Primeval creature, we apply the Primeval Rule:

> **The Primeval Rule**: To get the attack of a Primeval creature, first apply the Eldritch Rule to the attack of the Primeval creature's mother. Then take that attack

3.4. THE PRIMEVAL RULE

together with the attack of the Primeval creature's father, and apply the Bloodthirsty Rule to the two. The result is the attack of the Primeval creature.

The mother of a Primeval Schniftoo is a Fluftoom. Applying the Eldritch Rule to the Fluftoom's attack of (♟), we get (♟). The father of the Primeval Schniftoo is an Aarobak, with an attack of (≈). We thus apply the Bloodthirsty Rule to the two attacks of (♟) and (≈) to get (♟)+(≈):

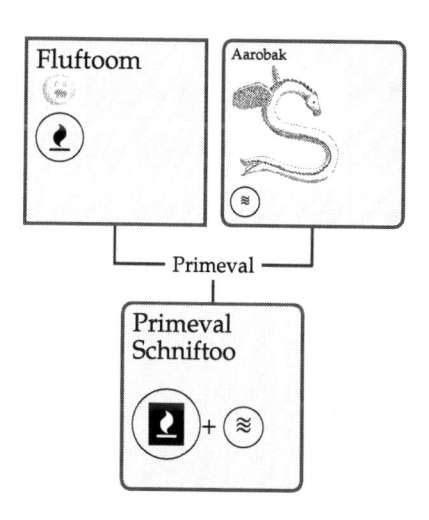

Fluftoom

Aarobak

Primeval

Primeval Schniftoo

Now that you're a master of the Bloodthirsty Rule and the Eldritch Rule, the Primeval Rule is just a matter of putting together the pieces. Of course, the details aren't always so easy. Let's try two more examples.

First, the Primeval Vrilvriktu:

88   CHAPTER 3. ATTACKS AND VULNERABILITIES

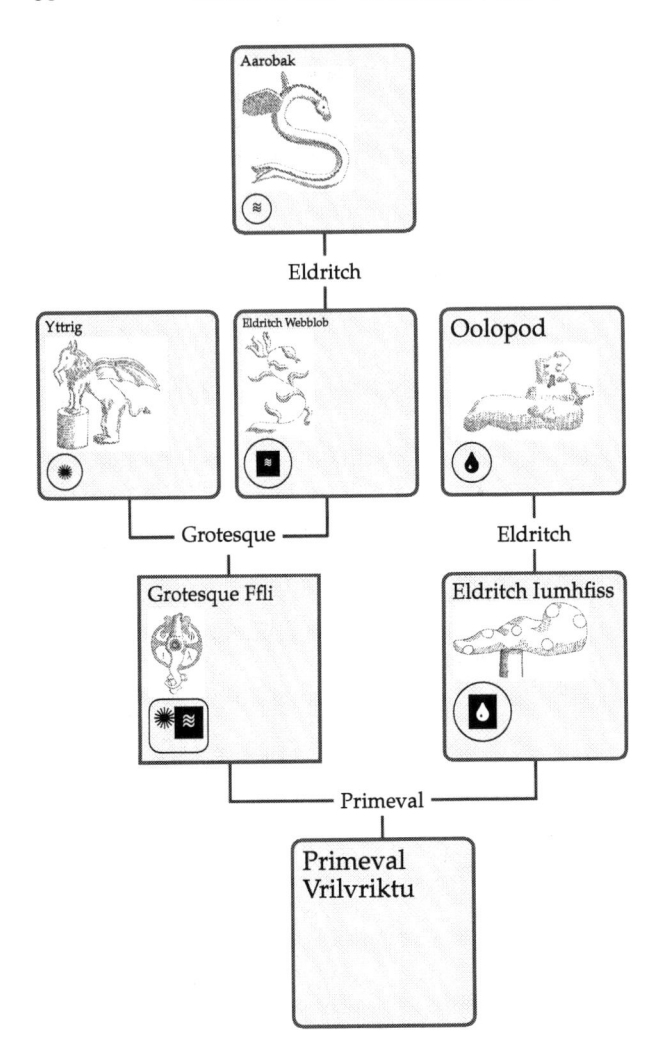

```
                    ┌──────────┐
                    │ Aarobak  │
                    │          │
                    │   [img]  │
                    │   (≈)    │
                    └────┬─────┘
                       Eldritch
     ┌────────────┬──────┴──────────┐
┌────┴───┐  ┌─────┴──────┐   ┌──────┴──────┐
│ Yttrig │  │Eldritch    │   │  Oolopod    │
│        │  │Webblob     │   │             │
│  [img] │  │   [img]    │   │    [img]    │
│   (✷)  │  │    (▦)     │   │     (◊)     │
└────┬───┘  └─────┬──────┘   └──────┬──────┘
     └── Grotesque ──┘           Eldritch
           ┌─────┴──────┐    ┌──────┴────────┐
           │Grotesque   │    │Eldritch       │
           │   Ffli     │    │  Iumhfiss     │
           │   [img]    │    │    [img]      │
           │  (✷)(≈)    │    │     (◊)       │
           └─────┬──────┘    └──────┬────────┘
                 └──── Primeval ────┘
                  ┌─────┴──────┐
                  │  Primeval  │
                  │  Vrilvriktu│
                  │            │
                  │            │
                  └────────────┘
```

Following the Primeval Rule, we need to apply the Eldritch Rule to the attack of the Grotesque Ffli, who is the mother of the Primeval Vrilvriktu. Applying the Eldritch Rule to ✷≈ give us (✷)+ (≈). We then apply the Bloodthirsty Rule to that power and to the elemental attack of the Eldritch Iumhfiss, who is the father of the Primeval Vrilvriktu. The Eldritch Iumhfiss has an attack of (◊),

3.4. THE PRIMEVAL RULE

so the Bloodthirsty Rule gives us a final result of (☀) + (≈) + (💧):

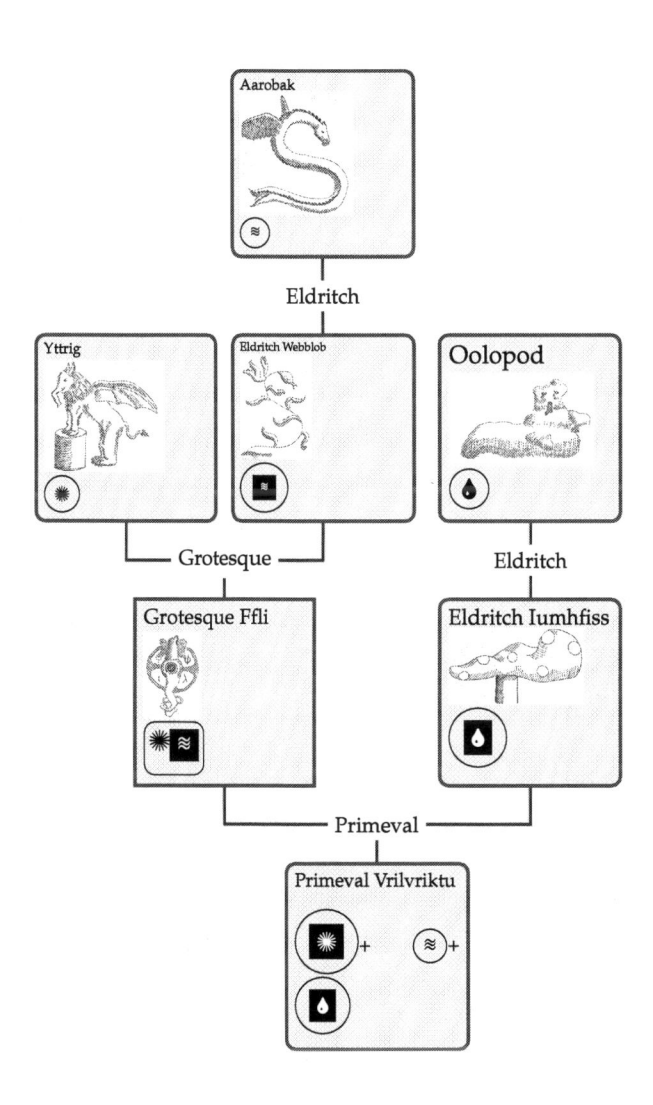

```
                    Aarobak
                    [drawing]
                      (≈)
                        |
                    Eldritch
       ┌────────────────┼────────────────┐
    Yttrig      Eldritch Webblob      Oolopod
   [drawing]      [drawing]          [drawing]
     (☀)            (▦)               (💧)
       └──── Grotesque ────┘     Eldritch
                |                    |
         Grotesque Ffli        Eldritch Iumhfiss
           [drawing]              [drawing]
            (☀)(≈)                   (💧)
                └──── Primeval ────────┘
                          |
                   Primeval Vrilvriktu
                    (☀) + (≈) +
                    (💧)
```

Second, the Primeval Achmemth:

90   CHAPTER 3. ATTACKS AND VULNERABILITIES

[Family tree diagram showing creature lineage with Aarobak at top, connected via Eldritch to a row containing Oolopod, Aarobak, Yttrig, Eldritch Webblob, and Oolopod. These connect via Primeval, Grotesque, and Eldritch relationships to Yttrig, Primeval J'jaklu, Grotesque Ffli, and Eldritch Iumhfiss. These further connect via Primeval lines to Primeval Gnomoloq and Primeval Vrilvriktu, which combine via Primeval into Primeval Achmemth at the bottom.]

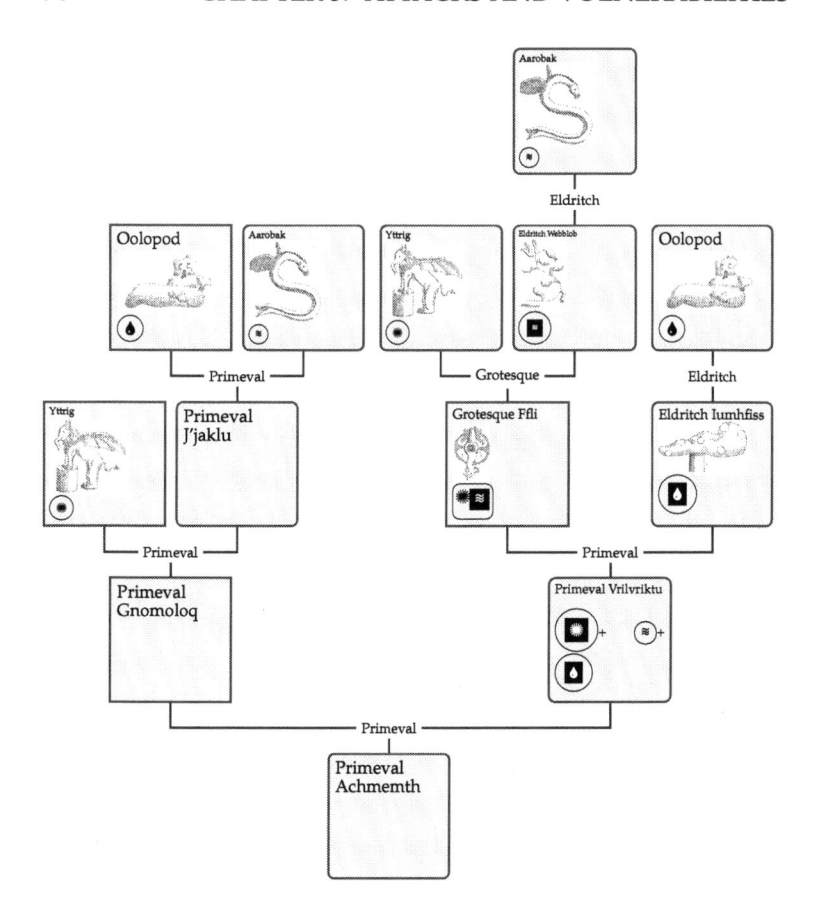

The Primeval J'jaklu is easy. We invert the water attack of its mother the Oolopod, and then pulse that (via the Bloodthirsty Rule) with the air attack of its father the Aarobak, to get $\left(\text{\large 💧}\right)$+ $\left(\approx\right)$.

And once we have the attack of the Primeval J'jaklu, the Primeval Gnomoloq is also easy. The mother of the Gnomoloq is the Yttrig, so we invert the Yttrig's attack to get $\left(\text{\large ☀}\right)$. Applying the Bloodthirsty rule to $\left(\text{\large ☀}\right)$ and the father Primeval J'jaklu's $\left(\text{\large 💧}\right)$+

3.4. THE PRIMEVAL RULE

≈), we have ✴ + ⬥ + ≈. Now we're ready to tackle the Primeval Achmemth itself:

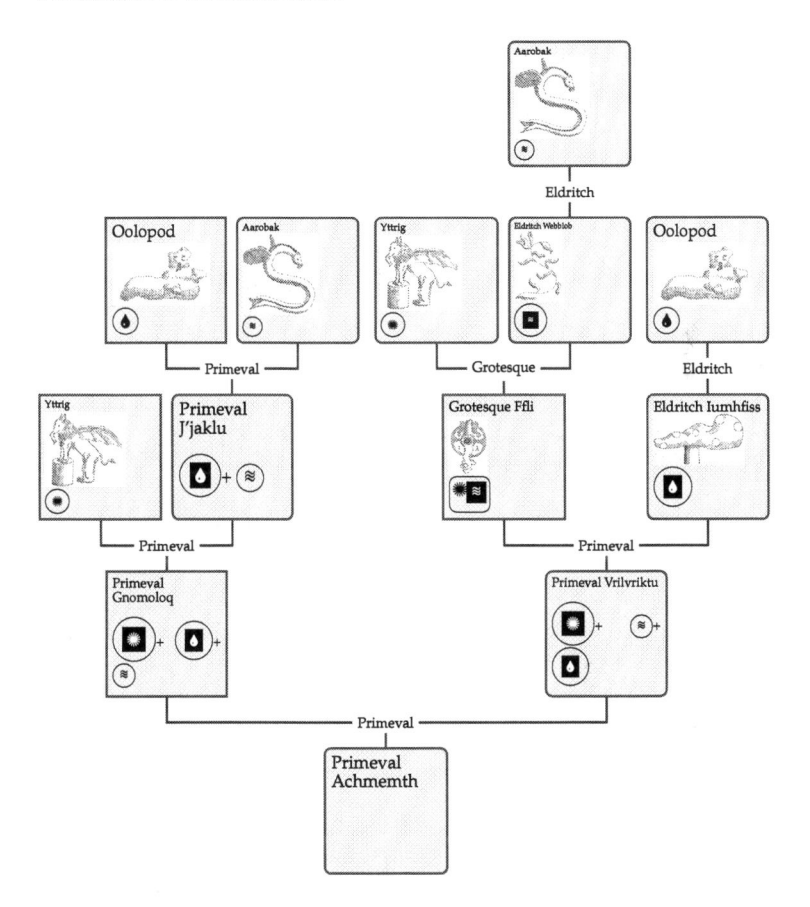

The first step is to apply the Eldritch Rule to the attack of the Primeval Gnomoloq (the mother of the Primeval Achmemth). Each element inverts, pulses become stacks, and stacks become pulses. So we need to stack ether, water, and dark air. We aren't stacking any pulsed attacks, so no need for the Box Method. It's just ✴⬥≈.

The second step is to take that result of ✴⬥≈, and then look at the attack of the Primeval Achmemth's father. That's the Primeval

Vrilvriktu, which we've already seen has an attack of (☀) + (≈) + (💧). So we put the two of these together using the Bloodthirsty Rule, which gives us (☀💧≈) + (☀) + (≈) + (💧). Our attack genealogy for the Primeval Achmemth is complete:

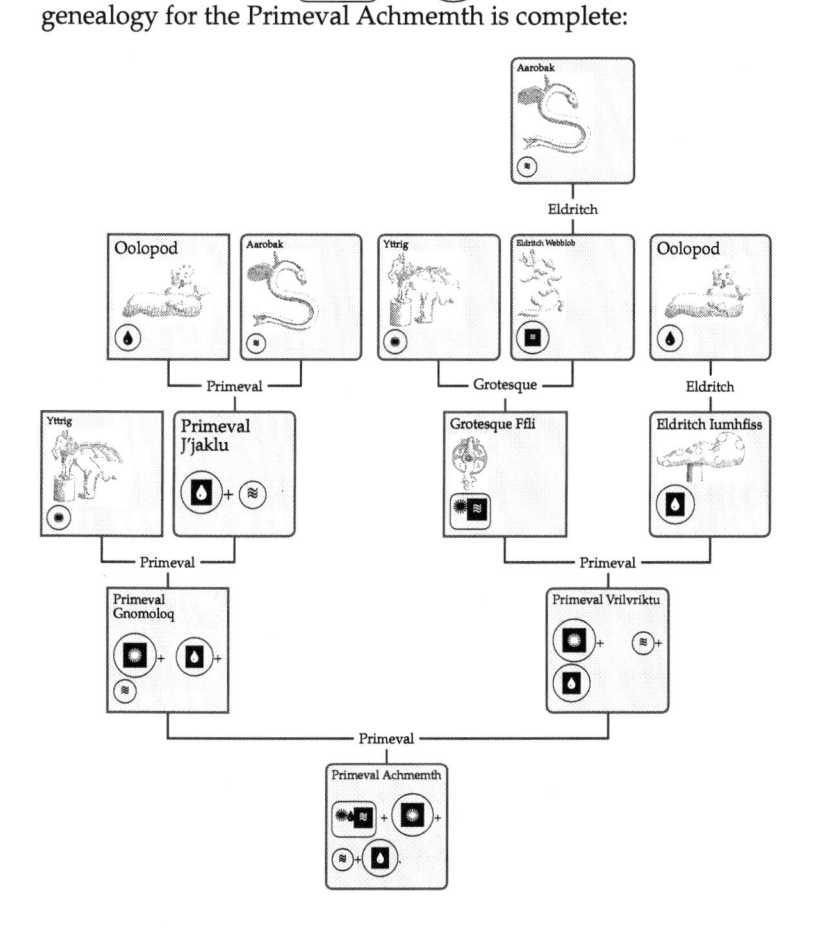

3.5 The Winged Rule

That leaves only the Winged creatures to deal with. Let's leap right into the Winged Rule, and then look at a few examples.

3.5. THE WINGED RULE

The Winged Rule: To determine the attack form of a Winged Logibeast, use the following steps:

1. Take the attack forms of the two parents of the Winged beast. Apply the Grotesque Rule to those two attacks to form a new attack that gets called in the business the *positive attack*.

2. Set aside the positive attack for now. Return to the attack forms of the two parents, and apply the Eldritch Rule to both of those attacks.

3. Combine the two Eldritch-modified attacks using the Grotesque Rule. Call the resulting new attack the *negative attack*.

4. Finally, combine the positive attack and the negative attack using the Bloodthirsty Rule. The result is the attack of the Winged creature.

So, let's try it out. Consider the Winged Hvornid:

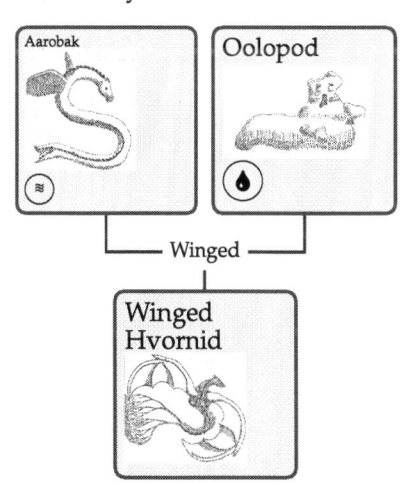

For the positive attack, we use the Grotesque Rule to combine the attacks of the parent Aarobak and Oolopod. That quickly gives us ≈◉.

To form the negative attack, we apply the Eldritch Rule to the parent attack powers. Since both of the parent attack powers are simple single elements, all we need to do to use the Eldritch Rule is to invert those two elements. That gives us (≈) and (◆). Combining those with the Grotesque Rule gives us the negative attack of ≈◆.

Finally, we combine the positive attack and the negative attack with the Bloodthirsty Rule, giving us ≈◆ + ≈◆. The Winged Hvornid uses an attack that alternates pulses of combined air and water with pulses of combined dark air and dark water.

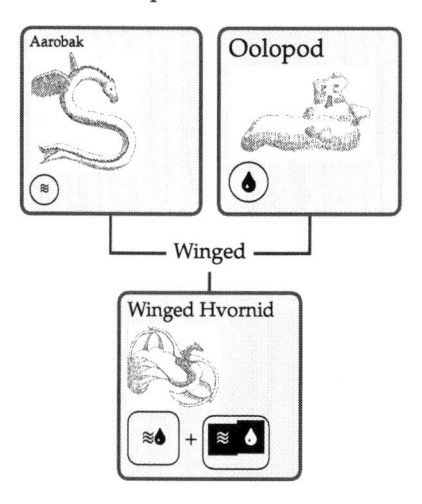

Aarobak | Oolopod
└── Winged ──┘
Winged Hvornid
≈◆ + ≈◆

Next let's try the Winged Xeerun:

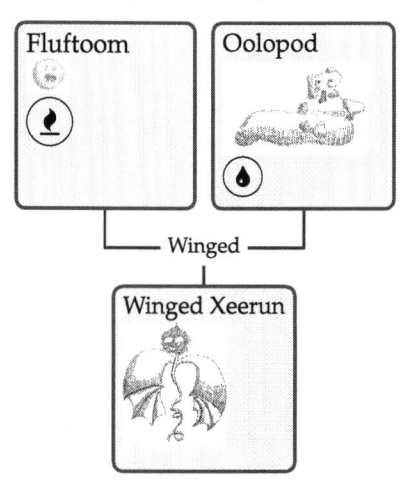

Fluftoom | Oolopod
└── Winged ──┘
Winged Xeerun

3.5. THE WINGED RULE

Determining the attack of the Winged Xeerun is much like determining the attack of the Winged Hvornid. The positive attack stacks the attacks of the parent Fluftoom and Oolopod, and is thus ⚡💧. To get the negative attack, we invert the elemental attacks of the parents, giving (⚡) and (💧). We then stack these with the Grotesque Rule to make ⚡💧. Then we combine the positive attack and the negative attack using the Bloodthirsty Rule to make the final Winged Xeerun attack of ⚡💧 + ⚡💧:

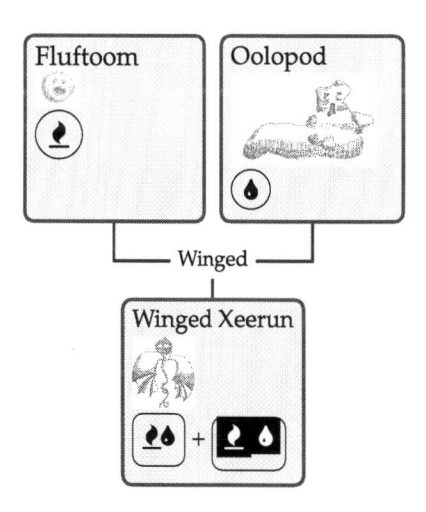

```
┌──────────┐  ┌──────────┐
│ Fluftoom │  │ Oolopod  │
│          │  │          │
│   ⚡     │  │   💧     │
└────┬─────┘  └────┬─────┘
     └──── Winged ──┘
           │
     ┌──────────┐
     │Winged Xeerun│
     │  ⚡💧 + ⚡💧 │
     └──────────┘
```

One more for practice. Let's work out the attack of the Winged Shugraat. As usual, we start with the family tree:

96 CHAPTER 3. ATTACKS AND VULNERABILITIES

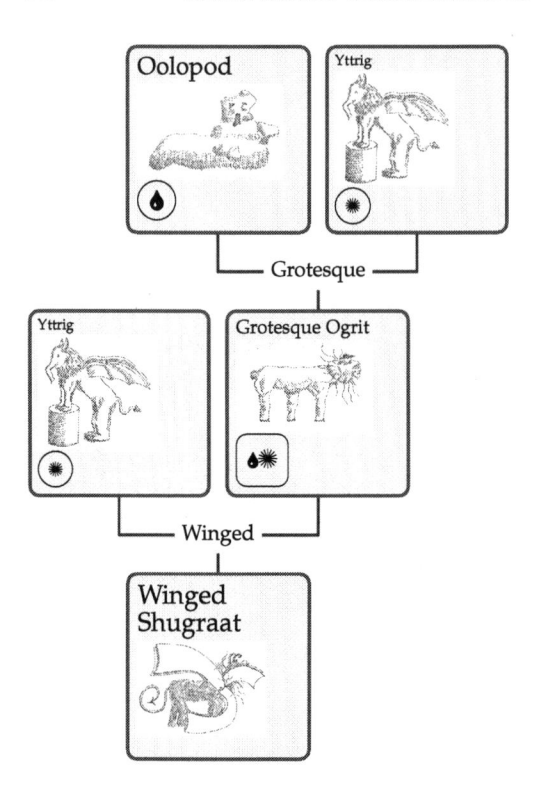

Now we apply the Winged Rule. The positive attack is easy: applying the Grotesque Rule, we stack ✹ (from the Yttrig parent) and 💧✹ (from the Grotesque Ogrit parent) to make 💧✹.

For the negative attack, we need to apply the Eldritch Rule to the attacks of both of the Winged Shugraat's parents. Appying the Eldritch Rule to the Yttrig's ✹ attack just inverts the element and gives us ✹. Applying the Eldritch Rule to the Grotesque Ogrit's 💧✹ attack *both* inverts the elements *and* changes the stacked attack into a pulsed attack, so we get 💧 + ✹.

Now we need to combine ✹ with 💧 + ✹ using the Grotesque

3.5. THE WINGED RULE

Rule. Since (💧) + (✳️) is stacked, we need to use the Box Method:

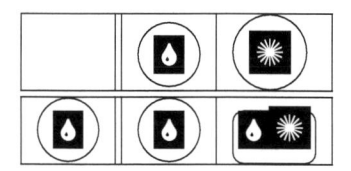

So the negative attack is (💧) + [💧✳️]. The last step is then to combine the positive and negative attacks using the Bloodthirsty Rule, which gives us [💧✳️] + 💧 + [💧✳️]:

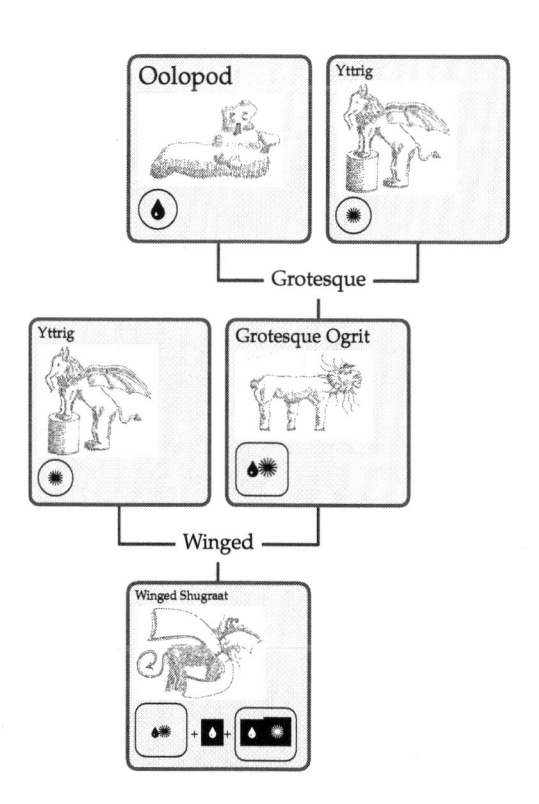

3.6 Logibeast Vulnerabilities

You now know all about Logibeast attacks – given even the most exotic of creatures (and a good supply of scratch paper) you can work out exactly what elemental attacks it launches. But that's not yet enough to bring success in the Logibeast arena. You also need to know what *affect* a beast's attacks will have on its component. A Fluftoom attacks with fire. A fire attack will wipe out a Bloodthirsty Awtroof, but it will bounce right off of an Oolopod and leave it unharmed. So even once you know how your Fluftoom attacks, you won't know everything you need to know in order to decide *when* to fight with a Fluftoom. You still need to master the fine (but quick!) art of Logibeast vulnerabilities.

Why does a fire attack destroy a Bloodthirsty Awtroof but not an Oolopod? It's because just as Logibeasts vary in what kind of elemental attacks they *use*, they also vary in what kind of elemental attacks they are *vulnerable to*. So before sending your beasts into combat, you'd better be able to work out what they (and their opponents!) are vulnerable to.

Oh, no – not another whole set of obscure rules! I'll still struggling to get used to those crazy attack power rules, we hear you say. (Literally – we've entered into a data sharing agreement with Amazon Alexa and Google Home.) But you're in luck. Once you've determined the attack of a Logibeast, you're 90% of the way to knowing its vulnerabilities, too. (We wish we could offer 100%. Early Logibeast duelists did act on the assumption that the vulnerabilities of a Logibeast are identical to its attacks, with some rather gruesome consequences when that assumption went wrong. It's not a bad approximation, but it can still go badly wrong at times. But keep your eyes open for forthcoming developments – Dutch researchers are working on an adequate genetic code for *Logibeests* which do have the same vulnerabilities as attacks.)

All you need to do, then, is master that last 10%. And it's easy. Vulnerabilities are determined from attacks almost exactly by applying the Eldritch Rule to the attack. The only (and crucial!) difference is that you *don't* invert the elements of the attack. In fact, let's make another rule out of that:

The Vulnerability Rule: Once you know the attack of

3.6. LOGIBEAST VULNERABILITIES

a Logibeast, to determine its vulnerability, apply the Eldritch Rule to its attack, but *without* inverting the elements. That is:

1. Change all of the stacked attacks into pulsed attacks, and all of the pulsed attacks into stacked attacks.
2. Use the Box Method to stack the resulting pulsed attacks.

That's it. You'll be a master in no time.

The best way to learn is by doing, so let's quickly work out the vulnerabilities of a few beasts.

First Example: Yttrig. The attack of a Yttrig, of course, is ether. Applying the Vulnerability Rule here is easy. There are no stacked attacks to change to pulsed attacks, and there are no pulsed attacks to change to stacked attacks. So nothing happens – the vulnerability of a Yttrig is also ether.

Yttrig:

- Attack: (✹)
- Vulnerability: (✹)

Second Example: Eldritch Webblob. It's the same deal. The attack of the Eldritch Webblob is dark air. Again, no stacked attacks and no pulsed attacks, so nothing for the Vulnerability Rule to do. Thus the vulnerability of the Eldritch Webblob is also dark air.

Eldritch Webblob:

- Attack: (≈)
- Vulnerability: (≈)

Third Example: Grotesque Gnuffle. The Grotesque Gnuffle attacks with the stacked attack 💧💧. To apply the Vulnerability Rule, we change that stacked attack into a pulsed attack. Because there are no pulsed attacks to change into stacked attacks, we don't need to use the Box Method to work out how to stack pulsed attacks. The result, then, is $(\text{\Large 🔥})+(\text{\Large 💧})$:

Grotesque Gnuffle:

- Attack: 🔥💧
- Vulnerability: $(\text{\Large 🔥})+(\text{\Large 💧})$

Fourth Example: Primeval Vrilvriktu. The Primeval Vrilvriktu attacks with the pulsed attack $(\text{\Large ✹})+(\approx)+(\text{\Large 💧})$. The Vulnerability Rule changes the pulsed attack into a stacked attack. Again there's no need for the Box Method, and we quickly get a vulnerability of ✹≈💧.

Primeval Vrilvriktu:

- Attack: $(\text{\Large ✹})+(\approx)+(\text{\Large 💧})$
- Vulnerability: ✹≈💧

Fifth Example: Winged Hvornid: So far we haven't had to use the Box Method, because we haven't consider a creature whose attack combines stacking and pulsing. But the Winged Hvornid will require the Box Method. The Winged Hvornid has an attack of ≈💧 + ≈💧. Applying the Vulnerability Rule, we change stacked attacks to pulsed attacks and pulsed attacks to stacked attacks. That means we get the two pulsed attacks:

- $(\approx)+(\text{\Large 💧})$
- $(\text{\Large ≈})+(\text{\Large 💧})$

We need to stack those two pulsed attacks, so time to pull out the Box Method again:

3.6. LOGIBEAST VULNERABILITIES

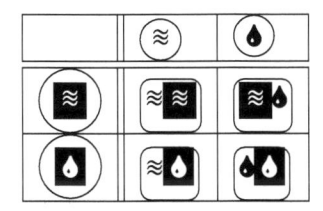

So we get a vulnerability of [≈≈] + [≈💧] + [≋💧] + [💧💧].

Winged Hvornid:

- Attack: [≈💧] + [≈ 💧]
- Vulnerability: [≈≈] + [≈💧] + [≋💧] + [💧💧]

Sixth Example: Eldritch Dkbaino. OK, one more example. Let's make it a really tricky one. The Eldritch Dkbaino, you may recall, has an attack of [⬢ ♟ 💧] + [♟ 💧] + [⬢ 💧]. That's three different stacked attacks all pulsed together. Applying the Vulnerability Rule, we'll then get three different *pulsed* attacks to be *stacked* together. The three pulsed attacks are:

- (⬢) + (♟) + (💧)
- (♟) + (💧)
- (⬢) + (💧)

Now we need to stack those together. Because there are three of them, we'll use the Box Method twice. (Rather than use a three-dimensional box.) First:

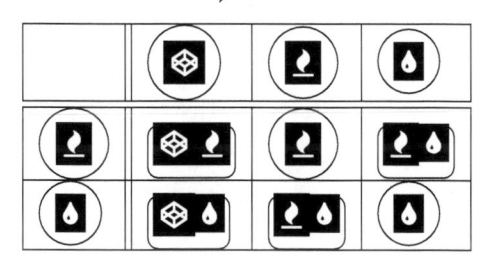

So from the first application of the Box Method, we get [⊕ ♪] + [♪ ♦] + [⊕ ♦] + (♪) + (♦). Now we need to stack this with the third pulsed attack of (⊕) + (♦), so we use the Box Method again.

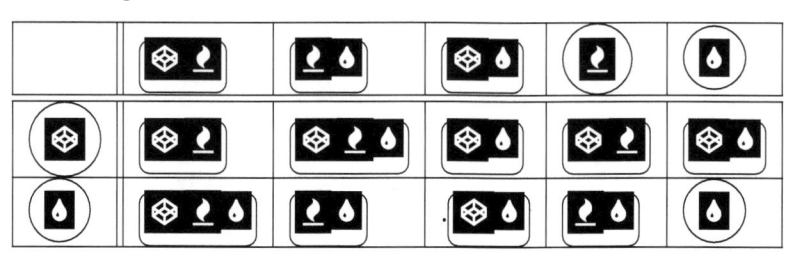

	[⊕ ♪]	[♪ ♦]	[⊕ ♦]	(♪)	(♦)
(⊕)	[⊕ ♪]	[⊕ ♪ ♦]	[⊕ ♦]	[⊕ ♪]	[⊕ ♦]
(♦)	[⊕ ♪ ♦]	[♪ ♦]	[⊕ ♦]	[♪ ♦]	(♦)

Putting it all together, we get a vulnerability of [⊕ ♪ ♦] + [⊕ ♪] + [⊕ ♦] + [♪ ♦] + (♦).

Eldritch Dkbaino:
- Attack: [⊕ ♪ ♦] + [♪ ♦] + [⊕ ♦]
- Vulnerability: [⊕ ♪ ♦] + [⊕ ♪] + [⊕ ♦] + [♪ ♦] + (♦)

3.7 Brief Review of Logibeast Elemental Theory

Let's assemble all the pieces in one place for easy reference. Given a Logibeast, the first step in working out its elemental attacks and vulnerabilities is to produce a family tree for the beast. We then work our way down the family tree filling in elemental attacks. The basic Logibeasts get their familiar attacks, and then in each subsequent generation we appeal to the appropriate phylum rule:

Bloodthirsty Rule	Bloodthirsty creatures always attack using a pulsing combination of their two parents' attack modes.

3.7. BRIEF REVIEW OF LOGIBEAST ELEMENTAL THEORY

Grotesque Rule	Grotesque creatures always attack using a stacked combination of their two parents' attack modes. (Using the Box Method as necessary to stack pulsed attacks.)
Eldritch Rule	Eldritch creatures always attack with an "inverted" version of their parent's attack, which changes elements to their anti-elements, stacked attacks to pulsed attacks, and pulsed attacks to stacked attacks. (Again using the Box Method as necessary to stack pulsed attacks.)
Primeval Rule	To get the attack of a Primeval creature, first apply the Eldritch Rule to the attack of the Primeval creature's mother. Then take that attack together with the attack of the Primeval creature's father, and apply the Bloodthirsty Rule to the two. The result is the attack of the Primeval creature.
Winged Rule	To determine the attack form of a Winged Logibeast, use the following steps: 1. Take the attack forms of the two parents of the Winged beast. Apply the Grotesque Rule to those two attacks to form a new attack that gets called in the business the *positive attack*. 2. Set aside the positive attack for now. Return to the attack forms of the two parents, and apply the Eldritch Rule to both of those attacks. 3. Combine the two Eldritch-modified attacks using the Grotesque Rule. Call the resulting new attack the *negative attack*. 4. Finally, combine the positive attack and the negative attack using the Bloodthirsty Rule. The result is the attack of the Winged creature.

Once you reach the bottom of the family tree, you'll have filled in the elemental attack form of the Logibeast you're interested in. You can then get the elemental vulnerability of that creature by applying the Vulnerability Rule to the attack form:

> **The Vulnerability Rule**: Once you know the attack of a Logibeast, to determine its vulnerability, apply the Eldritch Rule to its attack, but *without* inverting the elements. That is:
> 1. Change all of the stacked attacks into pulsed attacks, and all of the pulsed attacks into stacked

attacks.

2. Use the Box Method to stack the resulting pulsed attacks.

CHAPTER 4

DUELING WITH LOGIBEASTS

Attacks and vulnerabilities all worked out, it's time for a bit of the old ultraviolence. Let's send some Logibeasts into the arena and see who emerges victorious.

We'll start with a sample combat to show all the pieces in play, and then we'll summarize the steps. For our first official Logibeast combat, we'll pit a Yttrig against a Grotesque Ffli. In every Logibeast combat, one beast is the *champion* and one beast is the *challenger*. (That's the *past* champion, of course. And, as with stocks, past performance is no guarantee of future success – the challenger is just as likely to win as the champion is.) Let's have the Yttrig be the champion and the Grotesque Ffli be the challenger.

To have our beasts fight, we need to build an arena. A *scorekeeping* arena, that is, build with pencil and paper. (*Please* do not try to build your own actual combat arena. Logibeast combat should only ever occur in an official Logarena™, which comes with a number of safeguards built in to minimize risk to spectators.) The scorekeeping arena is always a rectangle. The champion is assigned the horizontal sides of the rectangle, and the challenger is assigned the vertical sides of the rectangle.

To build the arena, we need the attacks and vulnerabilities of both the champion and the challenger. These will then form the four walls of the arena, in the following manner:

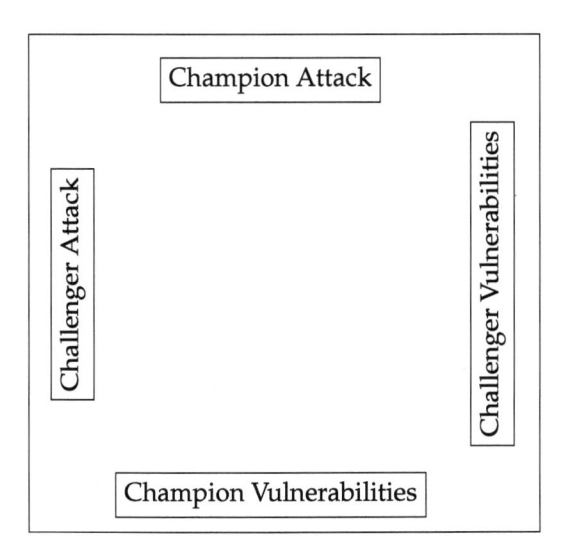

```
┌─────────────────────────────────────┐
│          ┌─────────────────┐        │
│          │ Champion Attack │        │
│          └─────────────────┘        │
│                                     │
│   ┌──┐                    ┌──┐      │
│   │Ch│                    │Ch│      │
│   │al│                    │al│      │
│   │le│                    │le│      │
│   │ng│                    │ng│      │
│   │er│                    │er│      │
│   │  │                    │Vu│      │
│   │At│                    │ln│      │
│   │ta│                    │er│      │
│   │ck│                    │ab│      │
│   └──┘                    │il│      │
│                           │it│      │
│                           │ie│      │
│                           │s │      │
│                           └──┘      │
│        ┌──────────────────────┐     │
│        │Champion Vulnerabilities│   │
│        └──────────────────────┘     │
└─────────────────────────────────────┘
```

To make the arena for the Yttrig versus Grotesque Ffli combat, we need the attacks and vulnerabilities of each. The Yttrig is easy: both attack and vulnerability are ether. The Grotesque Ffli attacks with stacked ether and dark air, so its vulnerability is (✺)+(≈). That lets us make the following arena:

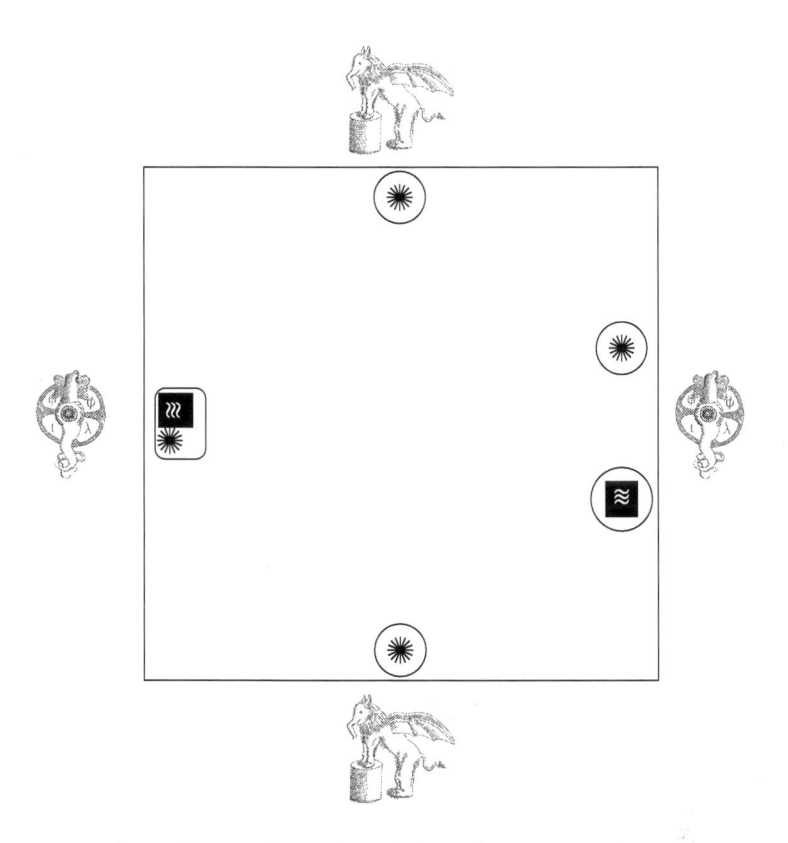

Notice that in listing the vulnerability of the Grotesque Ffli on the right, we don't bother with the '+' between the two pulsed components – we just list them out separately. Doing things that way turns out to make combat easier.

With the arena ready, it's time to track the combat in the arena. In the combat, we pit the attacks of the challenger against the vulnerabilities of the champion, and the attacks of the champion against the vulnerabilities of the challenger. There are two things you need to know about the combat. The first is the All-All Rule:

> **All-All Rule**: In order for a first beast to defeat a second beast in combat, *every* component of the attack of the first beast must exploit *every* component of the vulnerability of the second beast.

So for the Yttrig to defeat the Ffli, its attack of ✷ must exploit both the (☀) component of the Grotesque Ffli's vulnerability and the (≈) component of the Ffli's vulnerability. And for the Grotesque Ffli to defeat the Yttrig, its attack of [☀ ≈] must exploit the Yttrig's (only) vulnerability component of (☀).

But how does an attack component exploit a vulnerability component? For that, we need the Rule of Overlap:

> **Rule of Overlap**: An attack component exploits a vulnerability component if there is some element (dark or not) that is in *both* the attack component and the vulnerability component.

Let's see what the Rule of Overlap tells us about the tooth-and-claw battle between the Yttrig and the Grotesque Ffli:

1. The Yttrig attack component of (☀) (its only attack component) exploits the Grotesque Ffli vulnerability component of (☀), because they both contain (surprise!) the element of ether.

2. The Yttrig attack component of (☀) does *not* exploit the Grotesque Ffli vulnerability component of (≈), because there is no element that is common to the attack component and the vulnerability component. (Only ether in the one, only dark air in the other.)

3. The Grotesque Ffli attack component of [☀ ≈] exploits the Yttrig vulnerability component of (☀), because they both contain the element of ether. (The Grotesque Ffli attack component *also* contains the element of dark air, but that doesn't matter. As long as there is any elemental overlap between the two, the attack exploits the vulnerability.)

To carry out the combat, we'll add arrows showing what exploits what:

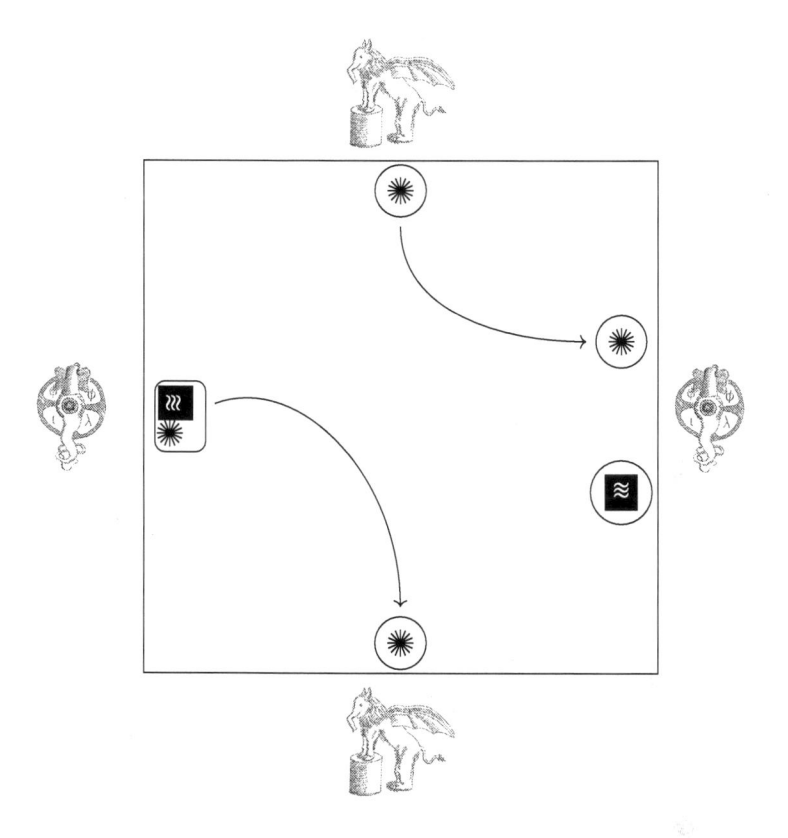

This arena now tells us the result of the combat, using the All-All Rule. Every component of the Grotesque Ffli's attack exploits every component of the Yttrig's vulnerability. (There is only one component of each, so the single arrow in the bottom left of the arena shows us all the exploiting we need.) But the Yttrig does not defeat the Grotesque Ffli, because not every component of the Yttrig's attack exploits every component of the Ffli's vulnerability – the ether attack component does not exploit the dark air vulnerability component.

Sometimes it's easier to see results – especially negative, fails-to-defeat, results – if we add additional arrows showing failures to exploit. We'll use dotted arrows for failures. Then we need to add a dashed arrow from the Yttrig's ether attack component to the Grotesque Ffli's dark air vulnerability component:

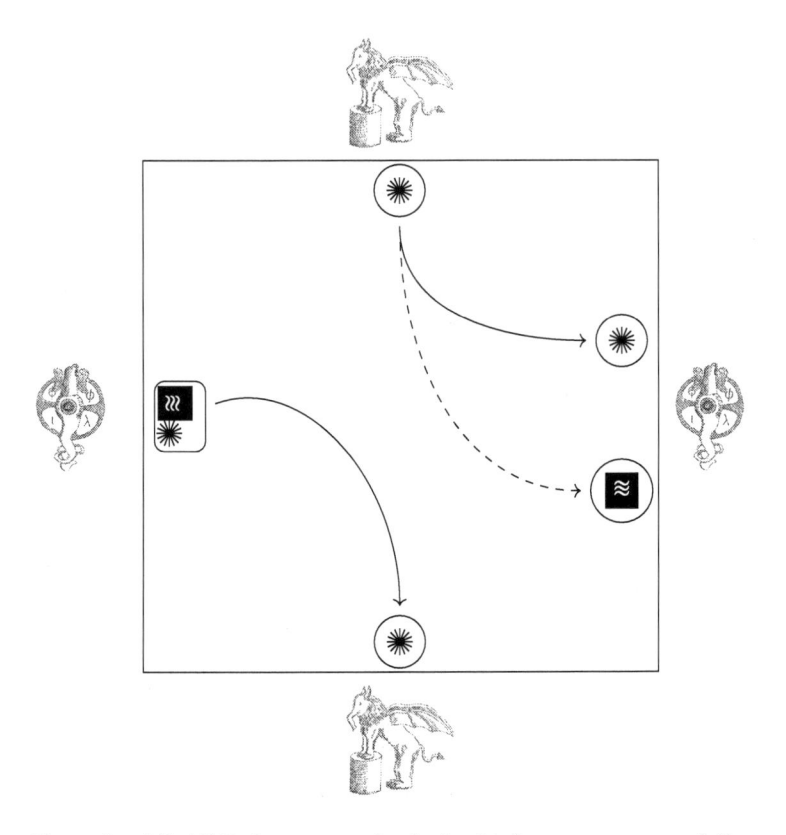

Given the All-All Rule, even a single dashed arrow means a failure to defeat. So since there's a dashed arrow from the champion to the challenger, the champion doesn't defeat the challenger. But there are no dashed lines from the challenger to the champion, so the challenger does defeat the champion. The Grotesque Ffli vanquishes the Yttrig – all hail the new champion.

There's our first combat done. Let's try another one, and then step back and talk about the technique more generally. This time, let's put a Primeval J'jaklu as a challenger up against a Bloodthirsty Azill champion.

The first step is to build the arena. For that, we need attacks and vulnerabilities for both creatures. We've already looked at the attacks for both:

- A Primeval J'jaklu has an attack of (💧)+(≈).

- A Bloodthirsty Azill has an attack of ⊕ + 🔥≈.

From these, we can determine the vulnerabilities:

- To get the vulnerabilities of the Primeval J'jaklu, we just change the pulsed attack into a stacked attack to get 💧≈.

- To get the vulnerabilities of the Bloodthirsty Azill, we need to stack earth with a pulsed attack of fire and air. That means the Box Method:

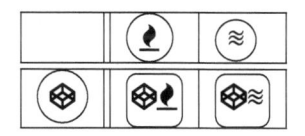

	🔥	≈
⊕	⊕🔥	⊕≈

So the vulnerability of the Bloodthirst Azill is ⊕🔥 + ⊕≈

OK, now we can build the arena. The champion Bloodthirsty Azill goes on the horizontal; the challenger Primeval J'jaklu goes on the vertical:

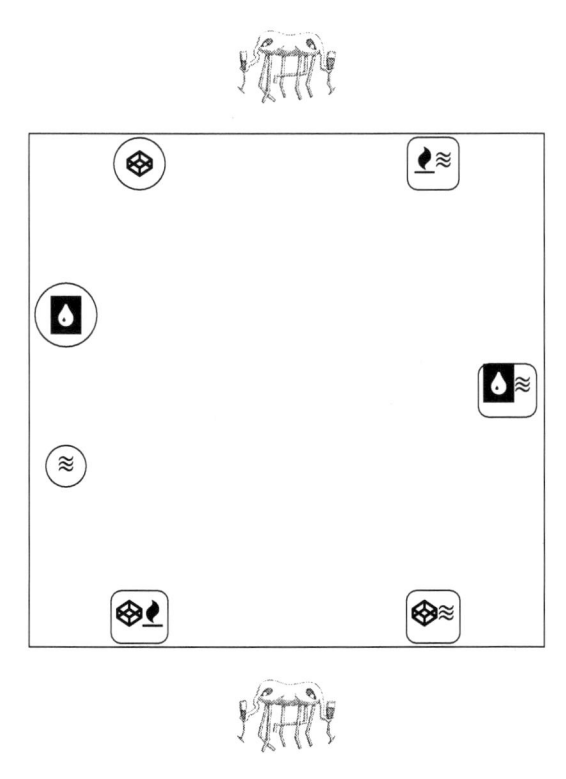

With the arena all prepared, let the combat begin! We draw in the exploiting arrows:

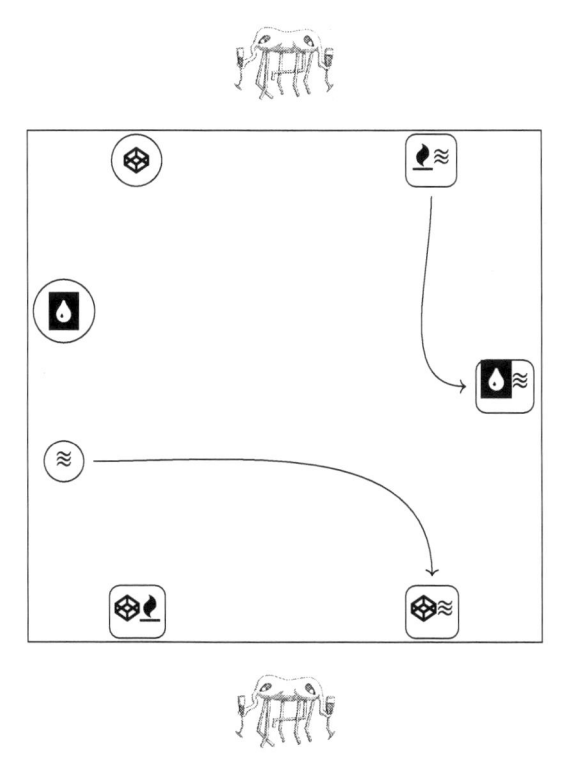

It's a draw! The challenger Primeval J'jaklu isn't able to defeat the champion Bloodthirsty Azill, because not every attack component of the J'jaklu exploits every vulnerability component of the Azill. (In fact, the Primeval J'jaklu does rather poorly. Its air attack component exploits only one of the two vulnerability components of the Bloodthirsty Azill - the ⊕≈ compknent, but not the ⊕⚫ compoent. And its dark water attack component doesn't exploit *either* component of the Azill's vulnerability.) And also, the champion Bloodthirsty Azill doesn't defeat the Primeval J'jaklu. Its attack component of fire stacked with air does exploit the Primeval J'jaklu's sole vulnerability component of dark water stacked with air (because of the overlap in air), but its other attack component of earth doesn't exploit the J'jaklu's vulnerability.

Again we can make this easier to see by adding the dashed failure arrows:

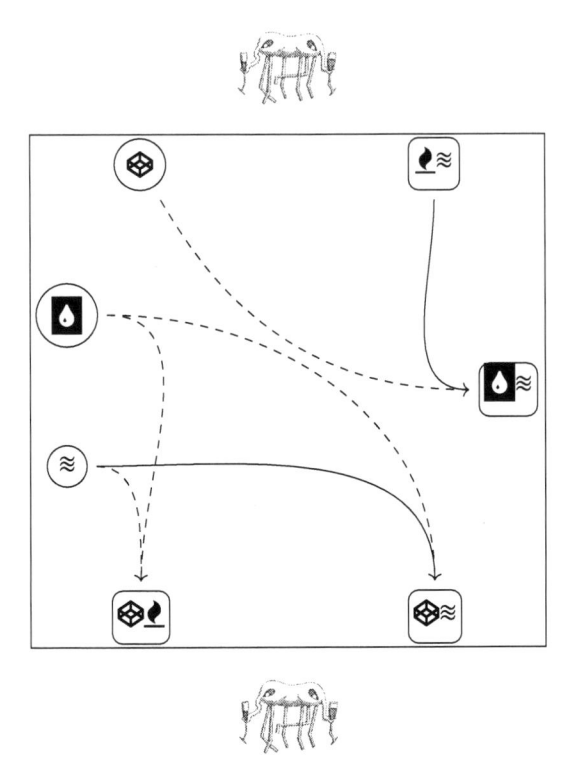

There are dashed failure arrows from challenger to champion and from champion to challenger, so everyone's attack fails. This combat is a draw – neither creature is able to harm the other.

4.1 Alpha and Omega

There's one final slight complication to deal with. When an element and its anti-element are brought together in a single attack component or vulnerability component, there are some unexpected effects.

Consider the innocent-looking Eldritch Whyndidid. As you'll remember (or re-calculate it if you don't!), the Eldritch Whyndidid has an attack of ⟨🔥🕯⟩. Its attack, that is, stacks fire and dark fire. That means its attack combines an element and its anti-element. When this happens, we invoke the Omega Rule:

4.1. ALPHA AND OMEGA

Omega Rule: An attack component that stacks an element with its anti-element is able to exploit *any* vulnerability component, even if the Rule of Overlap doesn't apply.

When an attack component contains both an element and its anti-element, it's common practice in designing the arena simply to replace that attack component with the symbol Ω, to remind ourselves that the Omega rule applies.

Let's see what happens when an Eldritch Whyndidid fights a Grotesque Ushtrimbot. The Eldritch Whyndidid attacks with 🝆🝇, so its vulnerability is (🝆) + (🝇). The Grotesque Ushtrimbot, as we worked out earlier, has an attack of 🝆💧✳≈, so its vulnerability is (🝆) + (💧) + (✳) + (≈). So let's make an arena:

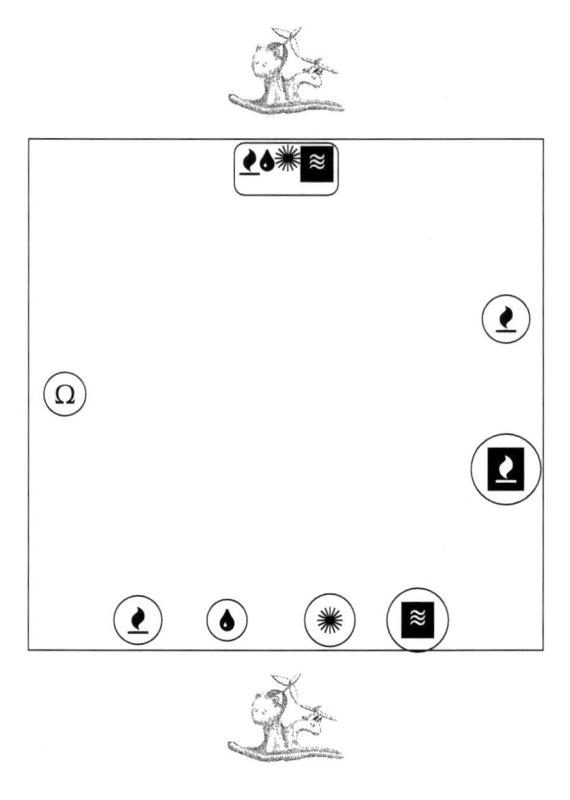

Let the combat begin! Let's add the arrows of exploitation:

4.1. ALPHA AND OMEGA

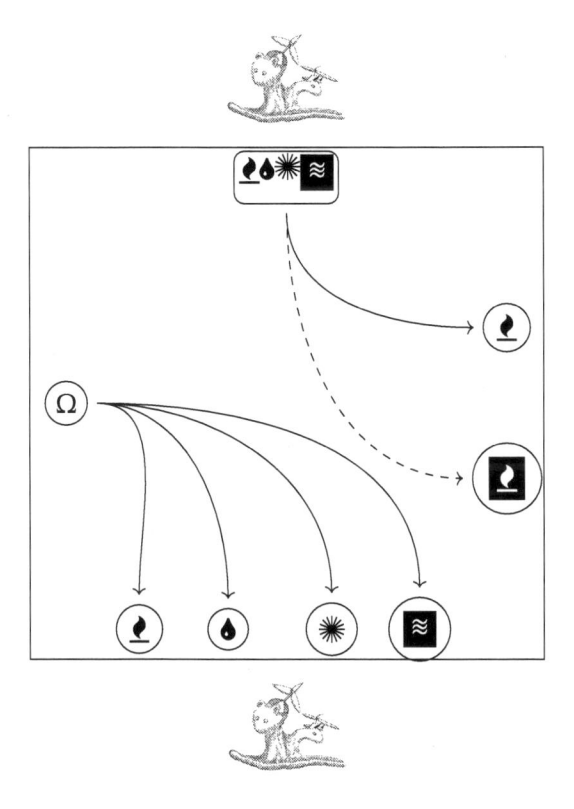

The Eldritch Whyndidid is victorious. Its Omega attack automatically exploits *all* of the Grotesque Ushtrimbot's vulnerability components, so it irresistibly defeats the Ushtrimbot. (Notice, in particular, that the Eldritch Whyndidid's Ω attack exploits the Grotesque Ushtrimbot's vulnerability component of 💧, even though the Eldritch Whyndidid's attack is really 🔥💧, which has no elemental overlap with 💧. That's the power of the Omega Rule – no elemental overlap is required when the Omega Rule applies.) Meanwhile, the Ushtrimbot's attack can exploit the fire vulnerability of the Eldritch Whyndidid, but not the dark fire vulnerability, so the All-All Rule isn't met, and the Grotesque Ushtrimbot can't defeat the Eldritch Whyndidid. (Notice the dashed arrow of failed exploitation.)

Wait, doesn't this mean that the Eldritch Whyndidid can defeat any-

thing? That's right. Because the Eldritch Whyndidid's only attack component is (Ω) and because (Ω) can exploit any vulnerability, it doesn't matter what creature you put up against the Whyndidid – the Whyndidid can always destroy it. (But that's not the same thing as saying that the Eldritch Whyndidid is *invulnerable* – more on that below.) For that reason, Eldritch Whyndidids are banned at all respectable Logibeast dueling events.

Two further notes about the Omega Rule:

1. As long as an attack component contains both an element and its anti-element, the Omega Rule applies and that attack component can be treated as (Ω). It doesn't matter if there are other elements in the component as well. ⊕✻⊗, for example, creates an Omega attack, because it contains both earth and dark earth. We can replace it with (Ω). It's okay to ignore the presence of ether in the attack component – because (Ω) already exploits everything, it doesn't matter whether we mention the presence of ether in the attack.

(But we do need to keep track of the presence of ether in the *vulnerabilities*. So use the Omega Rule on the attacks only *after* you've determined the vulnerabilities).

2. Consider the attack of the Winged Caicarx. Here's the family tree of the Caicarx:

4.1. ALPHA AND OMEGA

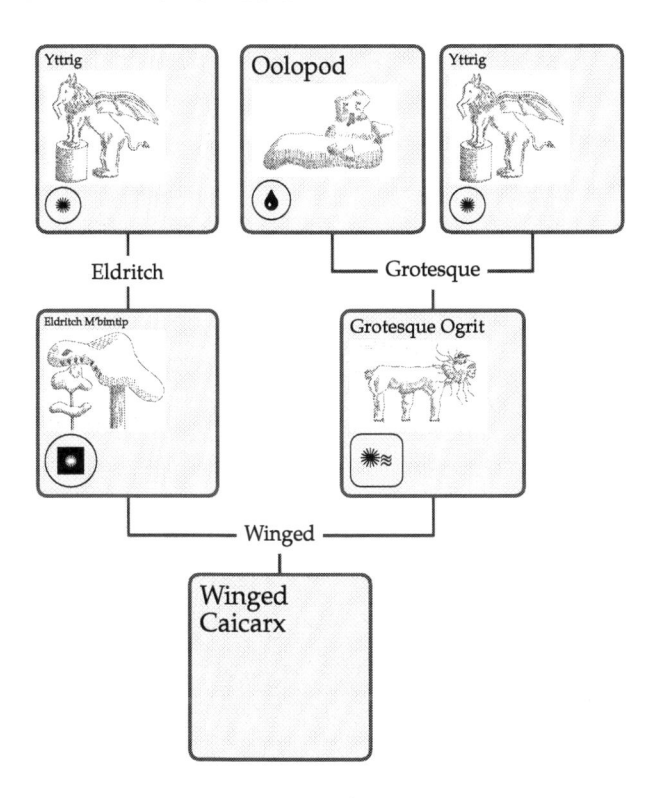

To find the attack of the Winged Caicarx, we use the Winged Rule, The positive attack is the stacking of the attacks of the Eldritch M'bimtip and the Grotesque Ogrit, or . To get the negative attack, we apply the Eldritch Rule to the attacks of the two parents. That gives us for the Eldritch M'bimtip and + for the Grotesque Ogrit. We then stack these using the Box Method:

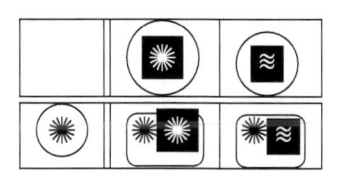

That gives us + . The attack of the Winged

Caicarx is thus ⬛ + ⬛ + ⬛.

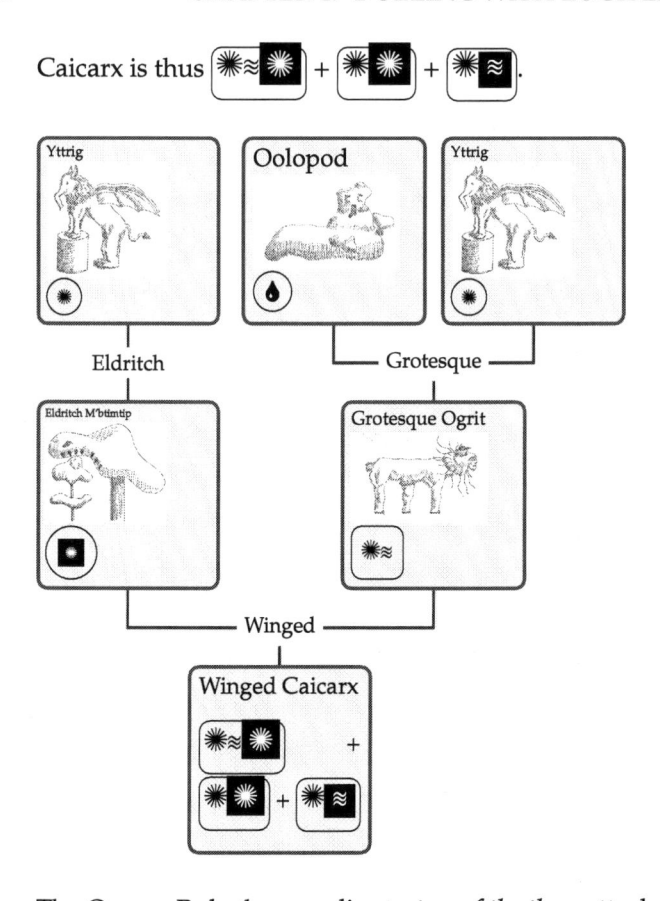

[Diagram showing creature lineage: Yttrig and Oolopod combine via "Eldritch" to form Eldritch M'btimtip; Oolopod and Yttrig combine via "Grotesque" to form Grotesque Ogrit; these combine via "Winged" to form Winged Caicarx.]

The Omega Rule then applies to *two of the three* attack components of the Winged Caicarx. The first attack component is ⬛. That contains ether and its anti-element dark ether, so we can replace it in the arena with (Ω). The second attack component is ⬛, which again contains ether and its anti-element dark ether, and can be replaced by (Ω). (There's no point in listing (Ω) more than once in the arena attacks of a given creature, by the way, so we can just put one (Ω) down for the Winged Caicarx.)

The (Ω) components of the Winged Caicarx's attack will exploit any vulnerability. But that's not enough to guarantee

4.1. ALPHA AND OMEGA

triumph for the Winged Caicarx. To defeat its opponent, *all* of its attack components must exploit all of the enemy vulnerability components. And the Winged Caicarx has that third attack component of ※≈ . For the Winged Caicarx to win, that component too must exploit all of the enemy's vulnerabilities. Just having an Omega attack somewhere in your attack capacities isn't enough to make you an unstoppable dueling machine.

So much for the Omega Rule. The Alpha Rule applies when a *vulnerability* component contains an element and its anti-element. Consider the Winged Hvornid. We've already worked out attacks and vulnerabilities for this beast:

- Attack: ≈💧 + ≈💧

- Vulnerability: ≈≈ + ≈💧 + ≈💧 + 💧💧

Notice that two of the vulnerability components of the Winged Hvornid contain an element and its anti-element. ≈≈ contains both air and dark air, and 💧💧 contains both water and dark water. To these two components we can apply the Alpha Rule:

> **Alpha Rule:** A vulnerability component that stacks an element with its anti-element can be exploited by any attack component, even if the Rule of Overlap doesn't apply.

Attacks that combine element and anti-element are particularly vicious attacks. Vulnerabilities that combine element and anti-element are particularly vulnerable vulnerabilities.

When a vulnerability component contains both an element and its anti-element, it's common practice in designing the arena to replace that vulnerability component with the symbol α, to remind ourselves that the Alpha Rule applies.

To see this in action, let's pit Winged Hvornid against Winged Hvornid. Here is the arena:

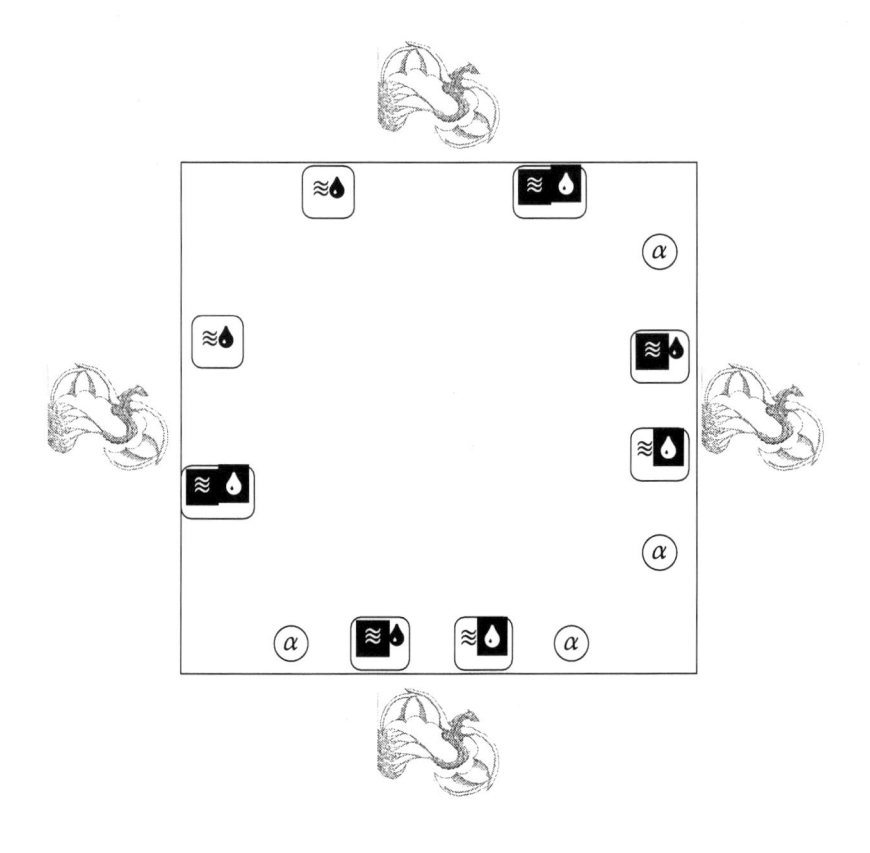

Now we add the exploitation arrows, remembering that the (α) vulnerability components are exploited by any attack:

4.2. THE THREE TRUE OUTCOMES

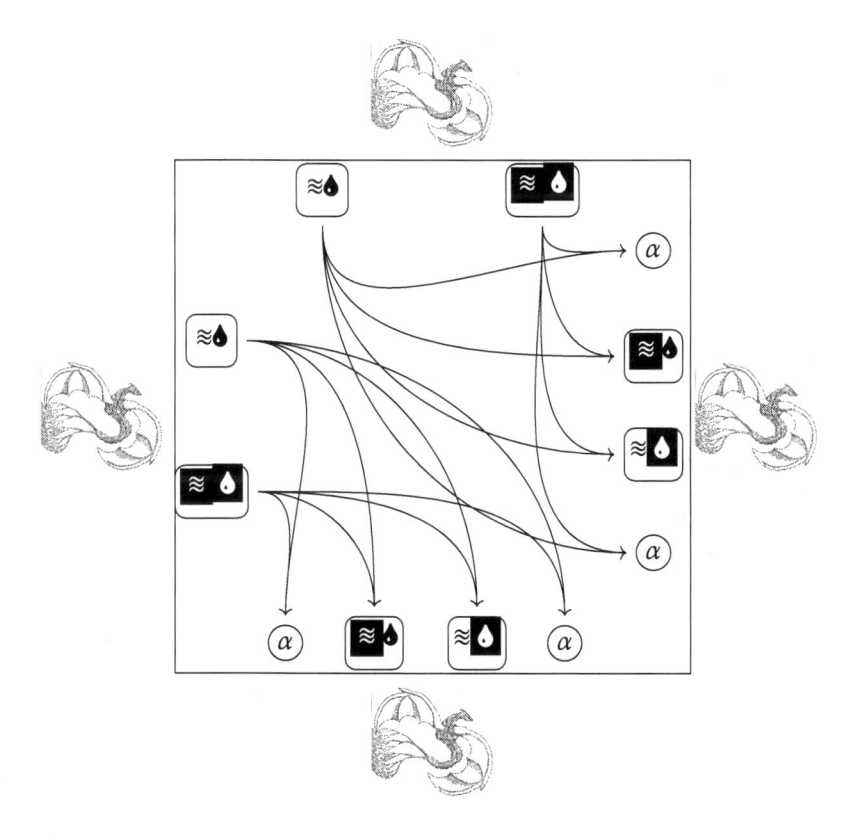

There are a lot of arrows to be parsed in that arena, but if you check carefully, you'll find that the All-All Rule has been met both by the champion Winged Hvornid and by the challenger Winged Hvornid. It's a destructive draw, with both creatures destroying each other. (Not a coincidence, as we've hinted earlier and will see in detail later.)

4.2 The Three True Outcomes

Having looked at some sample combats, it's time to be a bit more careful about scorekeeping and say what the final outcome of a combat can be. The core of the final outcome is the All-All Rule. There are four different situations you can find yourself in with this rule:

1. The champion Logibeast meets the All-All Rule, because all of its attack components exploit all of the challenger's vul-

nerability components, but the challenger Logibeast does *not* meet the All-All Rule, because at least one of its attack components fails to exploit at least one of the champion's vulnerability components.

2. The challenger Logibeast meets the All-All Rule, but the champion Logibeast does not meet the All-All Rule. (This is just the reverse of the previous case.)

3. Neither the champion nor the challenger Logibeast meets the All-All Rule. For both beasts, at least one of their attack components fails to exploit at least one of the vulnerability components of the opponent.

4. *Both* the champion *and* the challenger Logibeast meet the All-All Rule. Both beasts have all of their attack components exploit all of their opponent's vulnerability components.

The first two cases produce a clear winner. In the first case, the champion is victorious; in the second case, the challenger is victorious.

The third and fourth cases are draws, but draws of different sorts. The third case is called an *inconclusive draw*. Neither beast is able to harm the other, and the combat comes to nothing, with both beasts walking (flying, swimming, wriggling, burrowing, etc.) away unscathed. The fourth case is called a *destructive draw*. Both beasts are able to (and do!) harm the other, and the combat ends with two ex-Logibeasts.

These, then, are the three true outcomes of Logibeast duels: victory (for one side or the other), inconclusive draw, and destructive draw. We have in fact already seen examples of all three of these outcomes. Let's review them here:

1. **Victory: Grotesque Ffli versus Yttrig**

4.2. THE THREE TRUE OUTCOMES

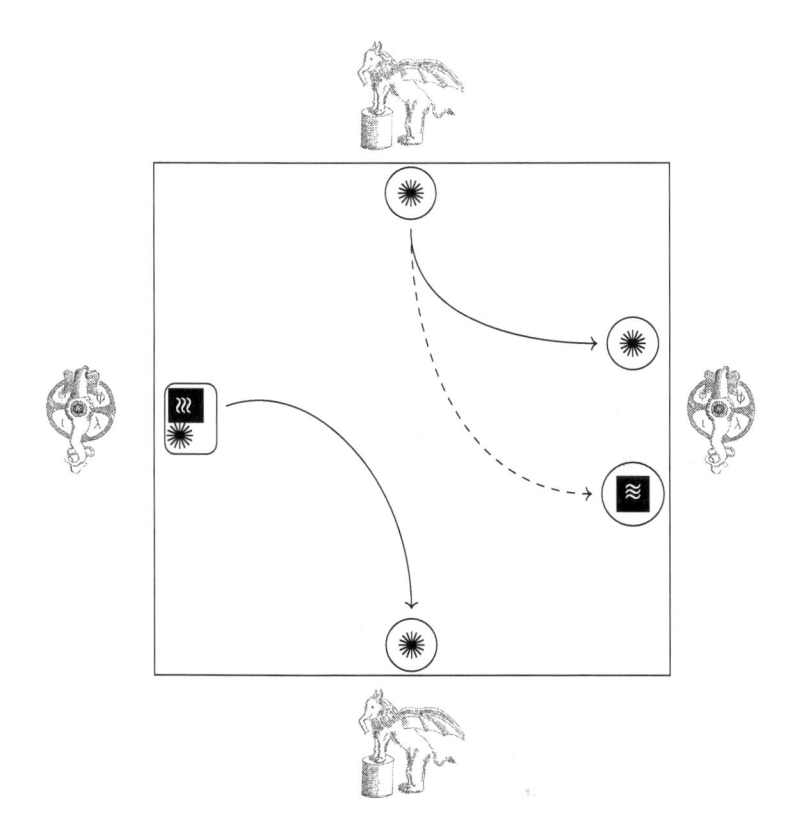

The Grotesque Ffli is victorious over the Yttrig.

2. **Inconclusive Draw: Primeval J'jaklu versus Bloodthirsty Azill**

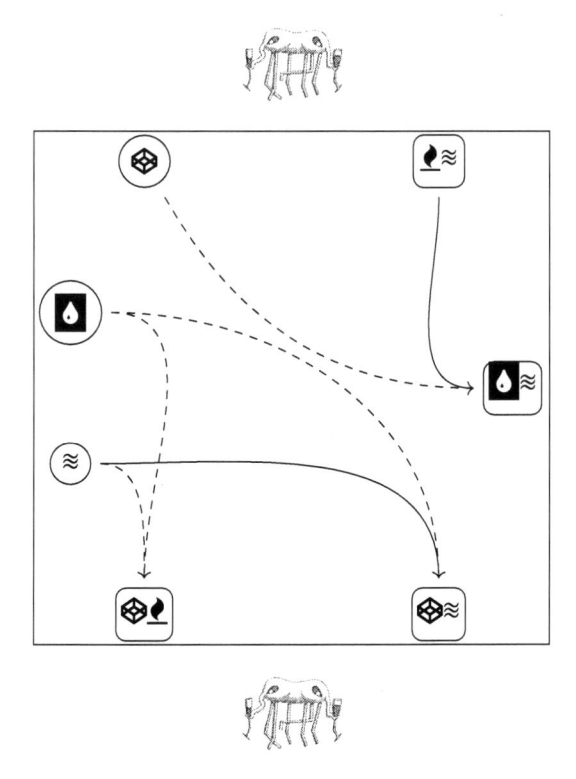

It's an inclusive draw. The Primeval J'jaklu is unable to harm the Bloodthirsty Azill, and the Bloodthirsty Azill is unable to harm the Primeval J'jaklu.

3. Destructive Draw: Winged Hvornid versus Winged Hvornid

4.2. THE THREE TRUE OUTCOMES

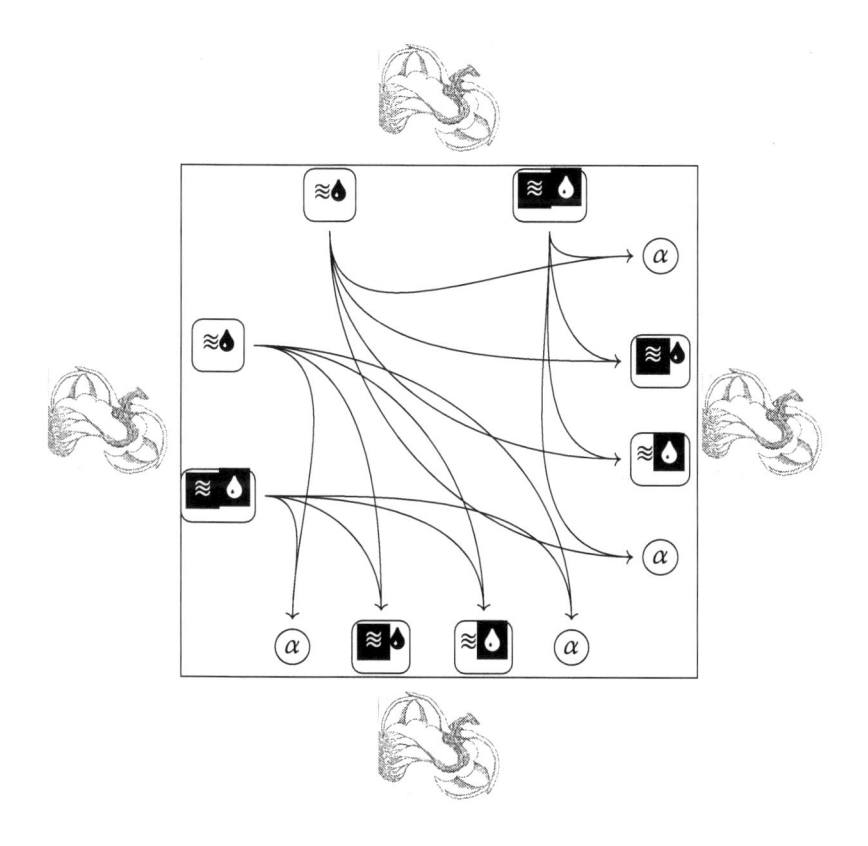

It's a destructive draw. The challenger Winged Hvornid is able to destroy the champion Winged Hvornid, but as that is happening, the champion Winged Hvornid also destroys the challenger Winged Hvornid.

We've mentioned that destructive draws are inevitable when two creatures of the same sort fight each other, but they can occur in other cases as well. For a really easy example, consider a fight between an Aarobak and an Eldritch Mumfloom. Both the Aarobak and the Eldritch Mumfloom have an attack of $(\approx)$ and a vulnerability of $(\approx)$, so the arena is very simple:

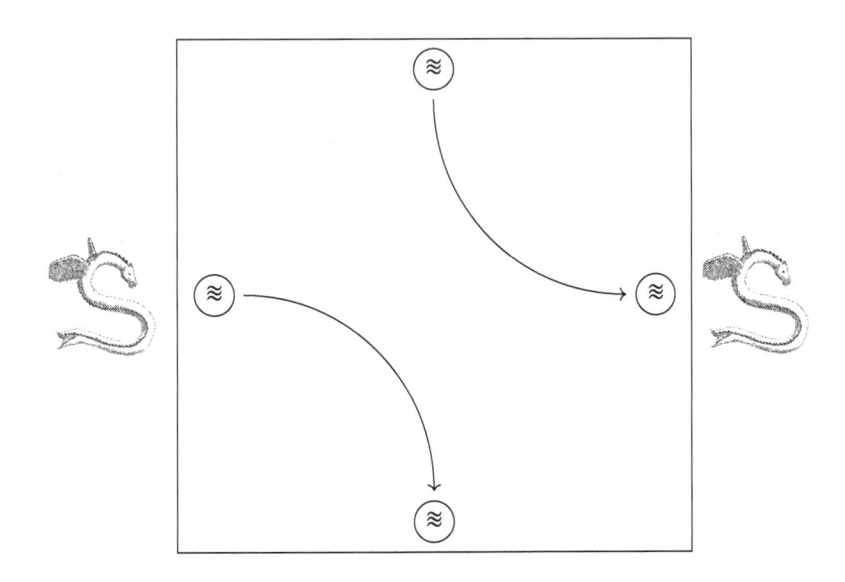

The Aarobak and the Eldritch Mumfloom destroy each other.

4.3 A Step-By-Step Guide to Logibeast Dueling

If you go to any respectable novice Logibeast combat tournament, you'll be given a checklist before every round, to help you navigate all the steps of the upcoming fight. Here's what the standard checklist looks like:

Combat Checklist

1. Determine the the identity of your creature (the challenger) and your opponent's creature (the champion).
2. Make a family tree for your creature, with the help of your Logibestiary.
3. Use the family tree to determine the attack form of your creature, applying the Grotesque, Blood-

thirsty, Eldritch, Primeval, and Winged Rules as necessary.

4. Use the Vulnerability Rule and the attack you've just determined to figure out the vulnerability of your creature.

5. Do the same for the opponent creature:
   (a) Make a family tree for the creature.
   (b) Use the family tree to work out the attack form of the creature.
   (c) Use the attack form to calculate the vulnerability of the creature.

6. Build a scorekeeping arena, with:
   (a) Your challenger beast's attack components along the vertical on the left.
   (b) Your challenger beast's vulnerability components along the vertical on the right.
   (c) The enemy champion beast's attack components along the horizontal at the top.
   (d) The enemy champion beast's vulnerability components along the horizontal at the bottom.

7. Look for attack components containing both an element and its anti-element and replace them with the Ω attack.

8. Look for vulnerability components containing both an element and its anti-element and replace them with the α vulnerability.

9. Draw in arrows of exploitation, remembering to use the Omega Rule to have Ω attacks exploit all vulnerabilities and to use the Alpha Rule to have α vulnerabilities be exploited by all attacks.

10. If you find it helpful, also draw in the dashed failed exploitation arrows.

11. Examine the arrows in the scorekeeping arena to determine whether the combat is a victory for the champion, a victory for the challenger, an inconclusive draw, or a destructive draw.

130 CHAPTER 4. DUELING WITH LOGIBEASTS

Let's do one more combat, walking through all of the steps in detail. You've brought your Grotesque Qeqesflon to the tournament, and you find yourself matched up against a Primeval Gtuftbak. What will happen?

We know the challenger (your Grotesque Qeqesflon) and the champion (the Primeval Gtuftabk), so step 1 is done. On to step 2. Here's a family tree for your Grotesque Qeqeslon

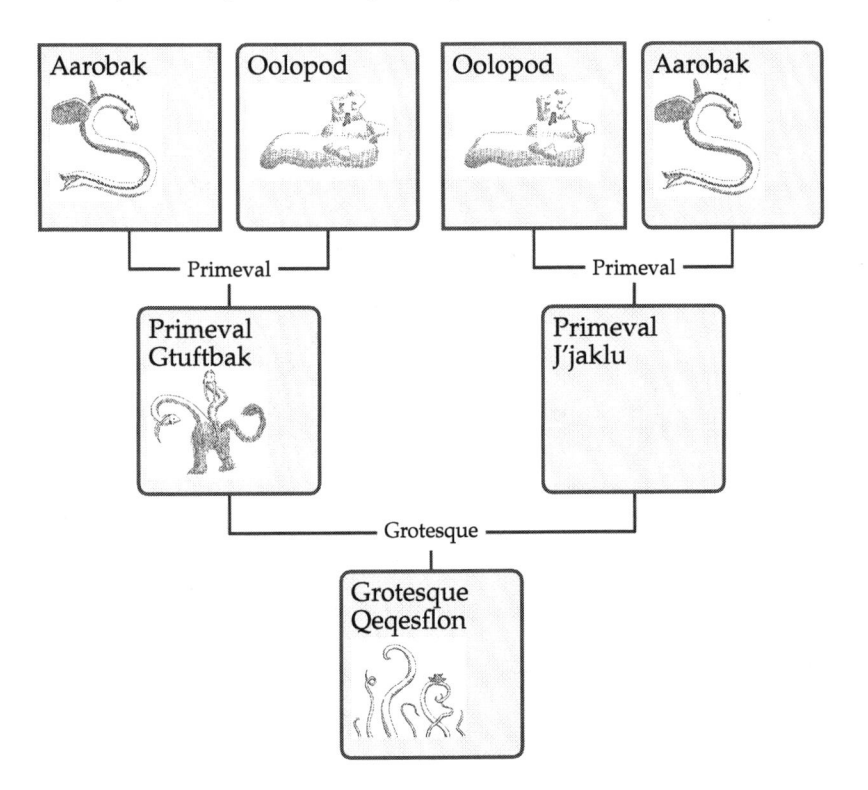

```
Aarobak   Oolopod       Oolopod   Aarobak
     └─ Primeval ─┘           └─ Primeval ─┘
      Primeval                  Primeval
      Gtuftbak                  J'jaklu
            └──────── Grotesque ────────┘
                    Grotesque
                    Qeqesflon
```

Now we calculate attacks along the family tree. The attacks of the Oolopod and Aarobak, of course, are well-known. We use the Primeval Rule to learn that the Primeval Gtuftbak has an attack of $(\approx) + (\blacklozenge)$ and the Primeval J'jaklu has an attack of $(\blacklozenge) + (\approx)$. To get the attack of the Grotesque Qeqesflon, we need to stack the attacks of the Primeval Gtuftbak and the Primeval J'jaklu. That means using the Box Method:

4.3. A STEP-BY-STEP GUIDE TO LOGIBEAST DUELING   131

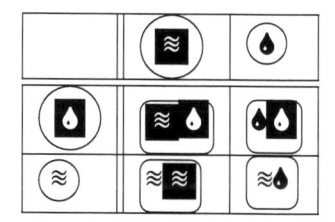

So the attack of the Grotesque Qeqesflon is [≈🌢] + [🌢🌢] + [≈≈] + [≈🌢]. Next we need the vulnerability of the Grotesque Qeqesflon. We convert the stacked attack components into pulsed components, giving us:

- (≈) + (🌢)
- (🌢) + (🌢)
- (≈) + (≈)
- (≈) + (🌢)

We now need to stack these four pulsed attacks, which means using the Box Method three times.

First we box (≈) + (🌢) and (🌢) + (🌢):

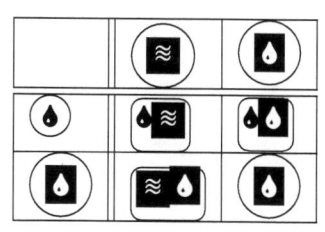

That gives us [🌢≈] + [🌢🌢] + [≈🌢] + (🌢). Next we box that with (≈) + (≈):

CHAPTER 4. DUELING WITH LOGIBEASTS

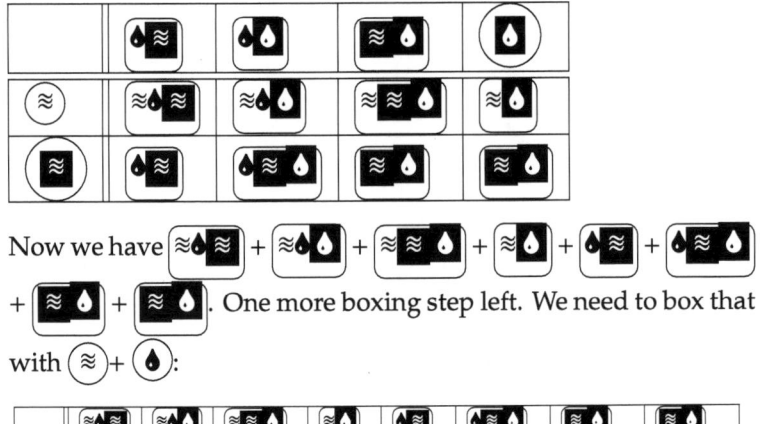

Now we have [≈◊□≈] + [≈◊■] + [≈■◊] + [≈■◊] + [◊■≈] + [◊≈◊] + [≈■◊] + [≈■◊]. One more boxing step left. We need to box that with (≈) + (◊):

That gives the Grotesque Qeqesflon the rather grotesque vulnerability of [≈◊■≈] + [≈◊■] + [≈■◊] + [≈◊] + [≈◊■] + [≈■◊] + [≈■◊] + [≈■◊] + [≈◊■] + [≈◊■] + [≈■◊] + [≈◊■] + [◊≈] + [◊■≈] + [≈◊■◊] + [≈◊■].

But things aren't quite so awful as they look. Because this is a vulnerability, we can apply the Alpha Rule, and replace any component containing both an element and its anti-element with the alpha vulnerability. There are a lot of such components here. We end up with (α) + [≈■◊] + [◊■≈]. That's a bit more manageable.

In the same way, we can condense the attack of the Grotesque Qeqesflon from [≈■◊] + [◊◊] + [≈≈] + [≈◊] to (Ω) + [≈◊] + [≈◊].

OK, now we know all about the Grotesque Qeqesflon:

- Attack: (Ω) + [≈◊] + [≈■◊]
- Vulnerability: (α) + [≈■◊] + [◊■≈]

The next step is to do the same thing for the reigning champion,

4.3. A STEP-BY-STEP GUIDE TO LOGIBEAST DUELING   133

the Primeval Gtuftbak. We start with the family tree:

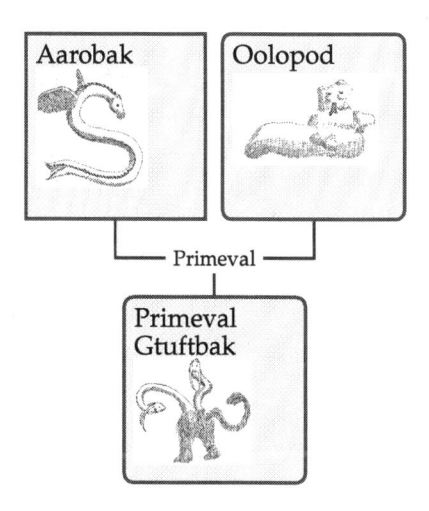

Aarobaks attack with air and Oolopods attack with water, so Primeval Gtuftbaks attack with ≈ + 💧. Their vulnerability is thus ≈💧.

On to step 6: time to build the scorekeeping arena. Your Grotesque Qeqesflon goes on the vertical, and the champion Primeval Gtuftbak goes on the horizontal:

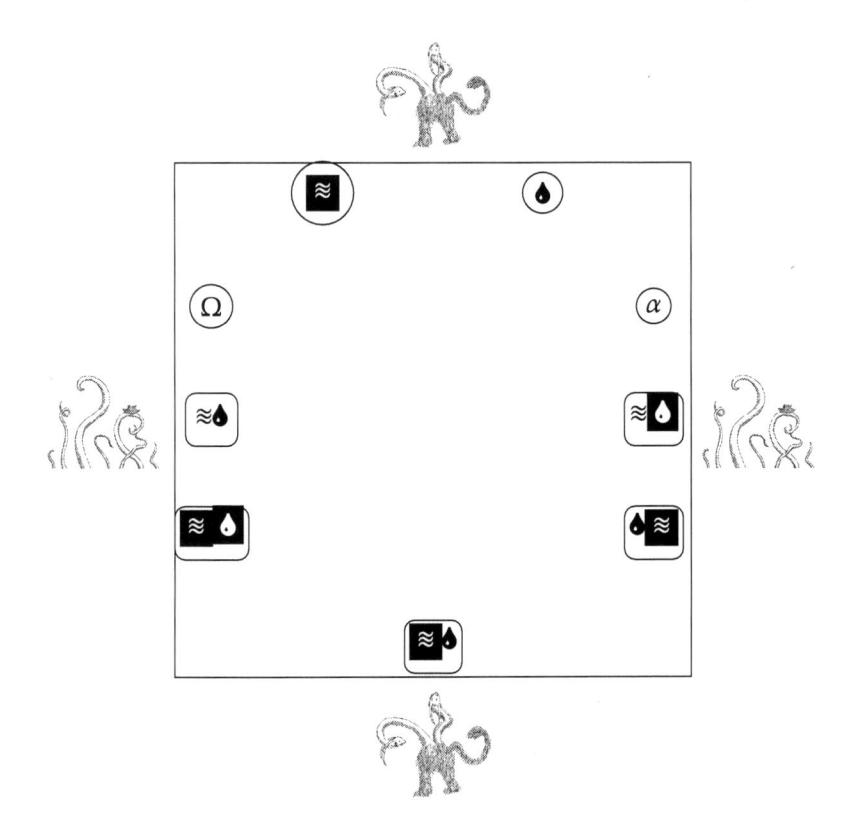

With the scorekeeping arena prepared, we begin the combat. We add the exploitation arrows, remembering that (Ω) defeats anything and that (α) is defeated by anything:

4.4. DESIGNER DUELING

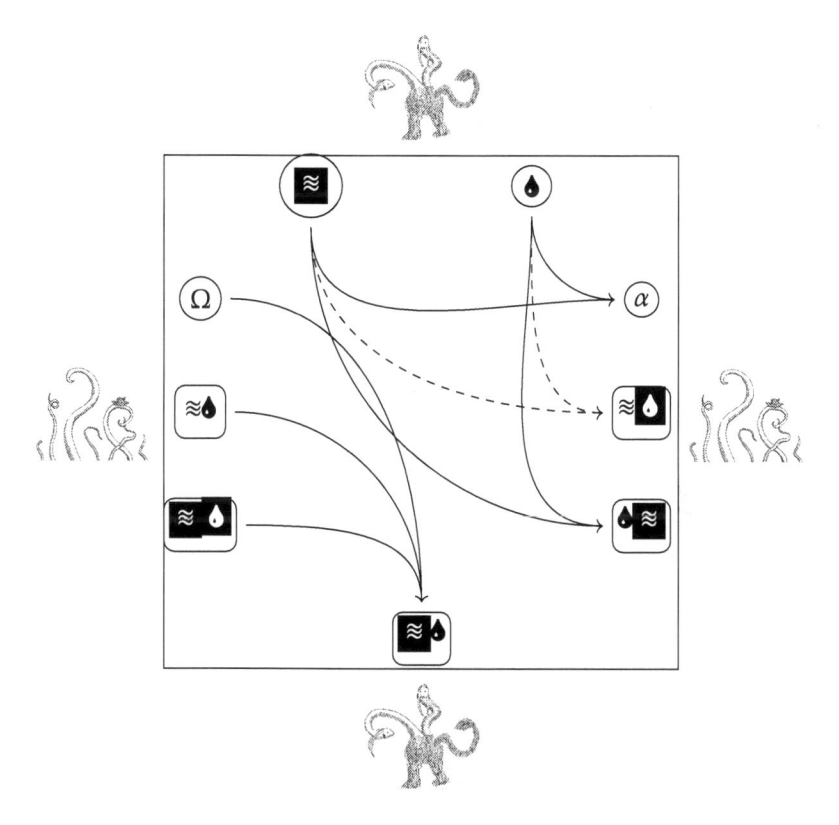

That brings us to the concluding step 11. Examining the arrows, we see that every attack component of your Grotesque Qeqesflon has exploited the one vulnerability of the Primeval Gtuftbak. (No dashed arrows!) However, both attack components of the Primeval Gtuftbak's attack fail to exploit one of your Qeqesflon's vulnerability (the ≈▲ component). As a result, it's a clean win for you. The Grotesque Qeqesflon is the new champion.

4.4 Designer Dueling

Logibeast combat is a tremendously popular sport, and many people are happy to spend their weekends bringing their favorite genetically engineered beasts to a local tournament and seeing how the creatures do in the arena. But for the true aficionados, *designer dueling* is the true sport – the place where subtle tactics complement the gratuitous violence of Logbeast combat.

In designer dueling, you don't come to the arena with Logbeasts at the ready. All you bring along is your Genetic Manipulator (and your own native wits). You're then given some eggs, and you have to first engineer a suitable creature with those eggs and then put that creature in the arena. Designer dueling adds an entire new dimension to Logibeast combat, since you need to plan ahead to work out the best beast to cook up.

.A whole new dimension, but nothing new in terms of genetic mechanics – everything that's new in the realm of designer dueling is in the area of tactics. And, frankly, it's just the job of a user's manual to teach you how to use all of the machinery, not to make you into a master strategian with the machinery. So we won't be having a lot to say about designer dueling – all we'll do here is give a brief overview of the typical format. (If you're out to improve your designer dueling, we highly recommend both *Four Weird Tricks With Your Genetic Manipulator* and *30 Days to a Better Dueling You*.)

Consider a sample designer dueling encounter. You've been given a Schloof egg and a Primeval Quiffex egg, and you're told to create a Logibeast to put in the arena against a Primeval Gtuftbak. You pull out your Genetic Manipulator and set to work:

Eggs	Step	Genetic Method	Input Creatures	Output Creature
(Schloof)	.1	Hatch	-	Schloof
(Primeval Quiffex)	2	Hatch	-	Primeval Quiffex
(Schloof, Primeval Quiffex)	3	Primeval Split	1,2	Grotesque Ogrit
(Schloof, Primeval Quiffex)	4	Grotesque Split	3	Oolopod

Or, pictorially:

Eggs	Step	Genetic Method	Input Creatures	Output Creature
(🦌)	.1	Hatch	-	🦌
(🐾)	2	Hatch	-	🐾
(🦌 , 🐾)	3	Primeval Split	1,2	🐾
(🦌 , 🐾)	4	Grotesque Split	3	🐾

Having whipped up a Oolopod from your Schloof and Primeval Quiffex eggs, it's time to put it to the test against the Primeval Gtuftbak.

4.4. DESIGNER DUELING

Oolopods attack with water, of course, so their vulnerability is also water. What about the Primeval Gtuftbak? Here's its family tree:

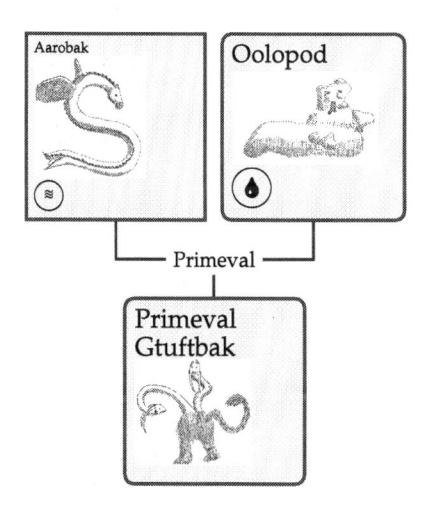

The attack of the Primeval Gtuftbak is then ($\approx$ + 💧), according to the Primeval Rule. Its vulnerability is $\approx$💧.

Now we have everything we need for an arena:

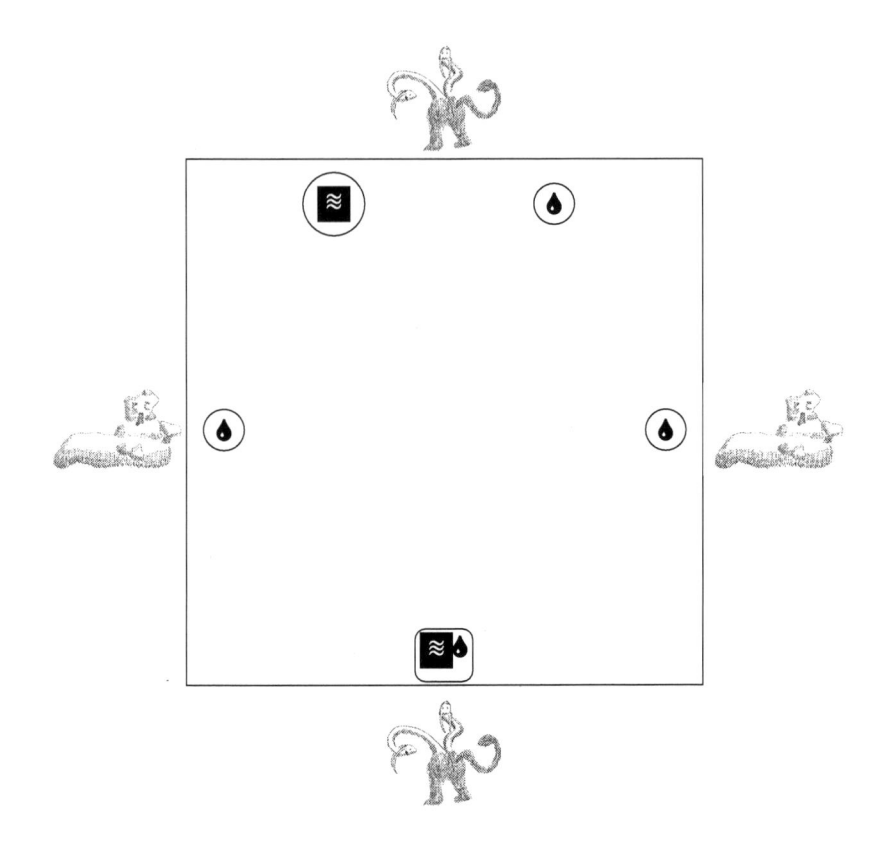

Arena in place, we let the combat begin, and draw in the exploitation arrows:

4.4. DESIGNER DUELING

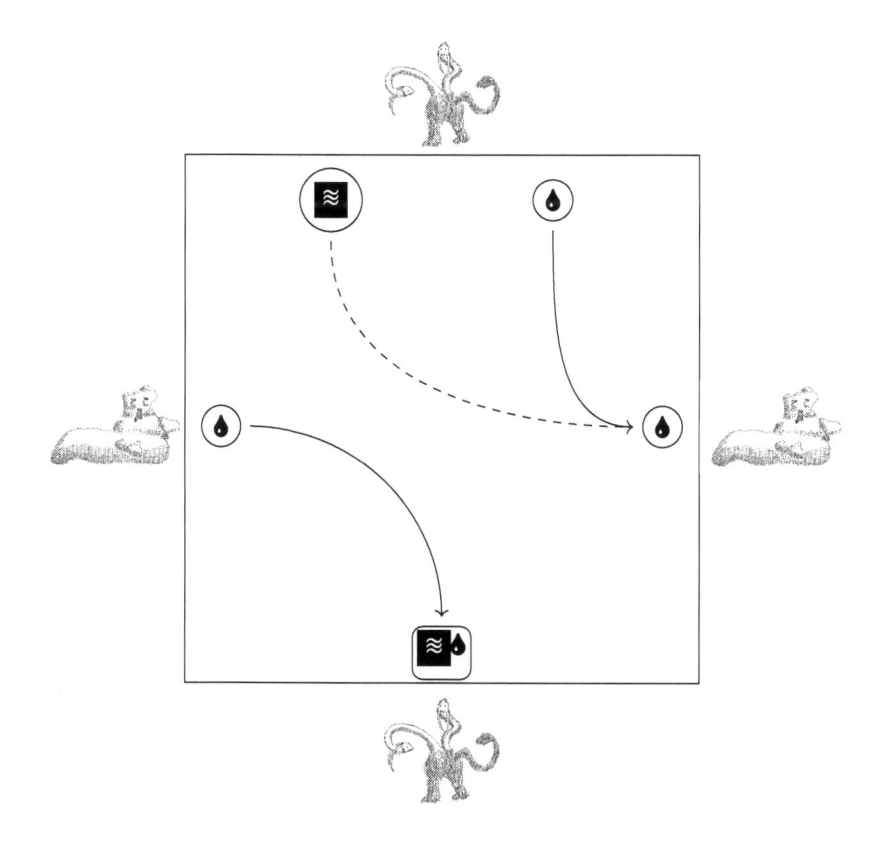

Your Oolopod satisfies the All-All rule and destroys the Primeval Gtuftbak, but the Primeval Gtuftbak's attack component of ≈ can't exploit your Oolopod's vulnerability. Victory for you, in your first foray into designer dueling.

Of course, they aren't all this easy. In harder matches, you may have to tinker for hours with your Genetic Manipulator to find the right recipe to produce a worthy fighter from your allotted eggs. (It's not uncommon, though, for designer dueling tournaments to have strict time limits on the genetic engineering phase of the event.) Here are a few further wrinkles that are common at designer dueling events:

1. **Family Restrictions**: You might be required, for example, to produce a Bloodthirsty creature from your eggs. If our previous example had been subject to that restriction, you

wouldn't have been able to send a Yttrig into combat, since it's not a Bloodthirsty creature. But with some cleverness you could still win. You could start with this recipe:

Eggs	Step	Genetic Method	Input Creatures	Output Creature
(Schloof)	.1	Hatch	-	Schloof
(Primeval Quiffex)	2	Hatch	-	Primeval Quiffex
(Schloof, Primeval Quiffex)	3	Primeval Split	1,2	Grotesque Ogrit
(Schloof, Primeval Quiffex)	4	Grotesque Split	3	Oolopod
(Schloof, Primeval Quiffex)	5	Bloodthirsty Merge	4	Bloodthirsty Waynhom

Or, pictorially:

Eggs	Step	Genetic Method	Input Creatures	Output Creature
(🐎)	.1	Hatch	-	🐎
(🐑)	2	Hatch	-	🐑
(🐎 , 🐑)	3	Primeval Split	1,2	🐐
(🐎 , 🐑)	4	Grotesque Split	3	🐛
(🐎 , 🐑)	5	Bloodthirsty Merge	4	

Now you have a Bloodthirsty Waynhom to send into the arena. That meets the requirement that your combatant be a Bloodthirsty creature. But how is it going to do in combat? Let's work out its attack. Here is the family tree of the Bloodthirsty Waynhom:

4.4. DESIGNER DUELING

```
                    ┌─────────┐
                    │ Aarobak │
                    │   🐍    │
                    │  (≈)    │
                    └────┬────┘
                      Eldritch
         ┌─────────┐   │  ┌──────────────┐
         │ Yttrig  │   └──│ Eldritch Web-│
         │   🐴    │      │ blob         │
         │  (✳)   │      │              │
         └────┬────┘      └──────┬───────┘
              └──── Grotesque ───┘
    ┌─────────┐         ┌──────────┐
    │ Oolopod │         │ Grotesque│
    │   🐻    │         │ Yazzil   │
    │  (💧)   │         │          │
    └────┬────┘         └────┬─────┘
         └──── Primeval ─────┘
              ┌───────────┐
              │ Bloodthirsty│
              │ Waynhom   │
              │           │
              └───────────┘
```

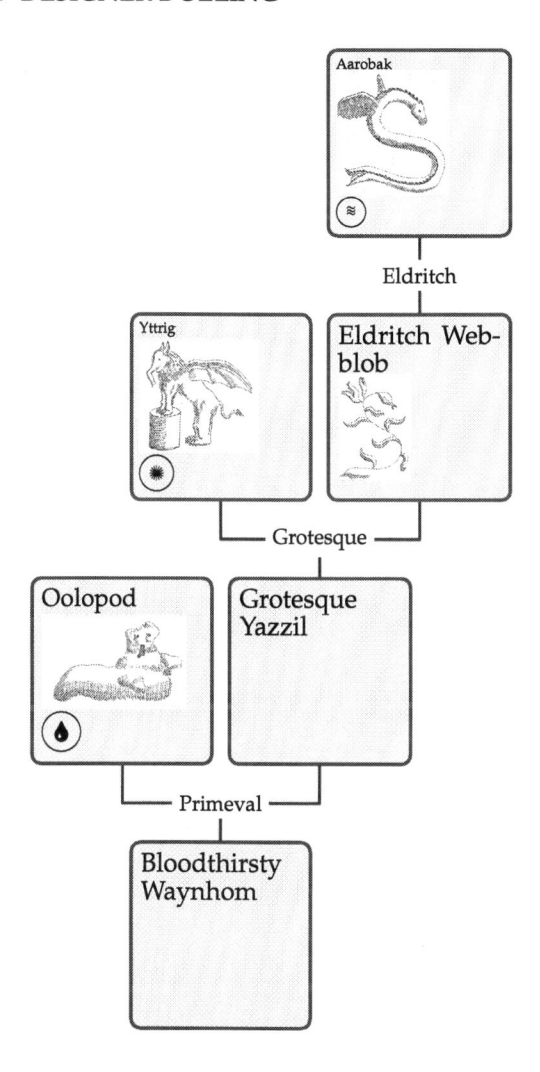

Working out way down the tree, the Eldritch Webblob has an attack of (≈), so the Grotesque Yazzil has an attack of [✳ ≈]. Thus the Bloodthirsty Waynhom has an attack of (💧)+[✳ ≈]:

142 CHAPTER 4. DUELING WITH LOGIBEASTS

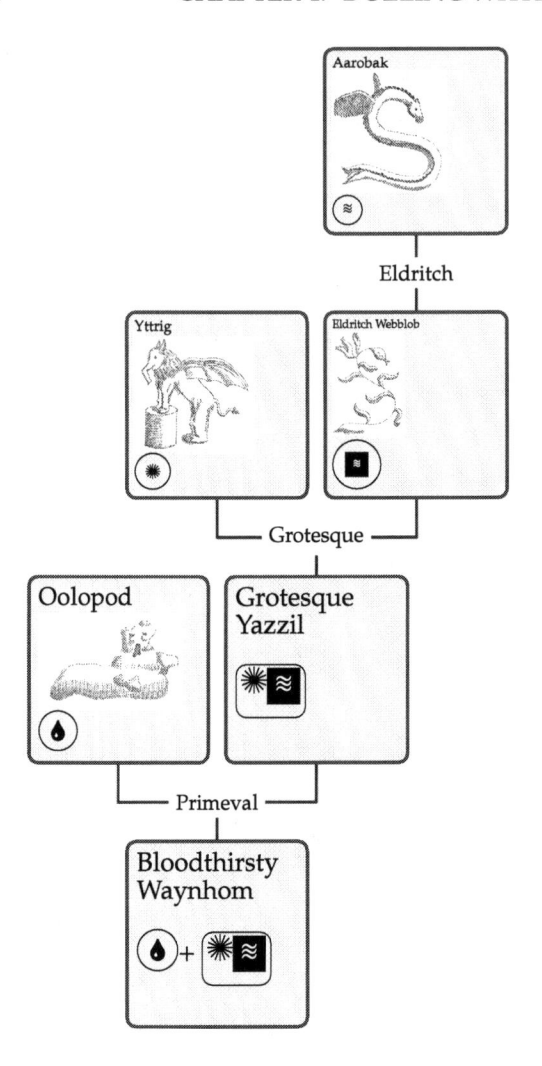

Next we need the vulnerability of the Bloodthirsty Waynhom. We need to stack (💧) with (✳) + (≈), which means it's time for the Box Method again:

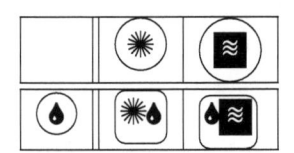

4.4. DESIGNER DUELING

The Bloodthirsty Waynhom's vulnerability is thus [💥💧] + [💧≈].

Next we make an arena in which the Bloodthirsty Waynhom will challenge the Primeval Gtuftbak (remembering from before that the Primeval Knug's attack is (≈)+ (💧) and its vulnerability is [≈💧].):

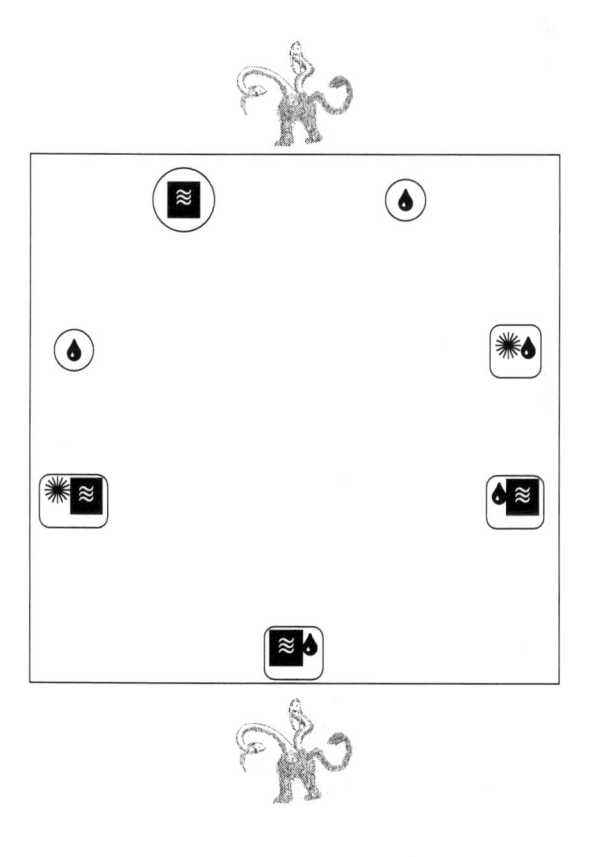

And now, the combat:

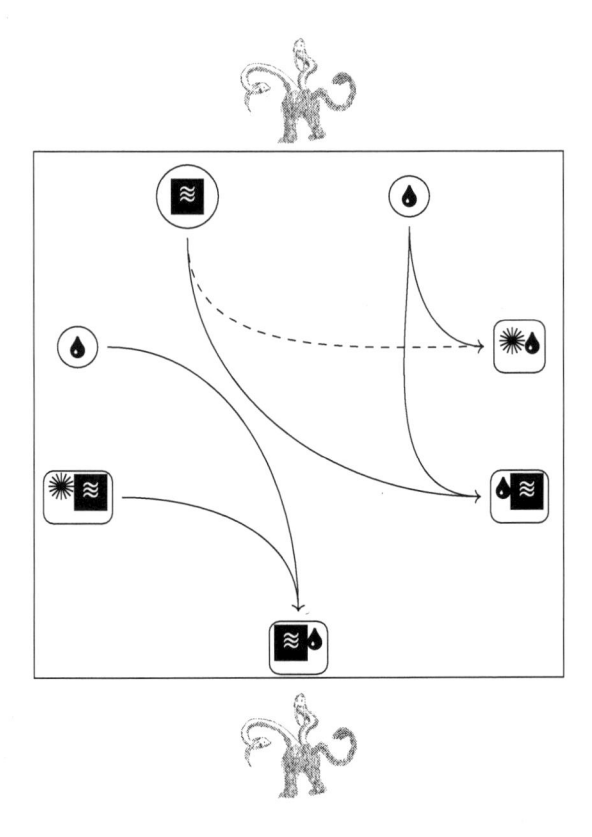

Both of your Bloodthirsty Waynhom's attack components exploit the one vulnerability of the Primeval Gtuftbak. However, one of the Primeval Gtuftbak's attack components (the ≈ component) fails to exploit one of the vulnerabilities of your Bloodthirsty Waynhom (the ☀♦ component). Thus your Bloodthirsty Waynhom is triumphant over the Primeval Gtuftbak.

Family restricted designer dueling calls for extensive familiarity with all of the genetic engineering methods of Logibeasts, so that you can make creatures of the appropriate attacks and vulnerabilities in whatever genetic family you are restricted to by the tournament rules.

2. **Power Class Restrictions**: Another common restriction method

4.4. DESIGNER DUELING

is to require you to engineer a creature that can defeat your opponent without being *too* strong. Suppose again you're given the Schloof and Primeval Quiffex eggs, and told to make a creature to face a Primeval Gtuftbak in the arena. But now there's a new rule: whatever creature you produce must not be able to defeat a Bloodthirsty Sweeftiq.

You can make (as we saw above) an Oolopod, which can defeat a Primeval Gtuftbak. Unfortunately, an Oolopod can also defeat a Bloodthirsty Sweeftiq. To see this, let's run the combat. Here's the family tree for a Bloodthirsty Sweeftiq:

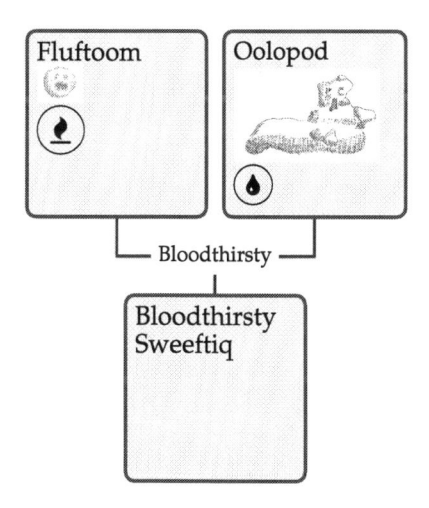

This is an easy one. The attack of the Bloodthirsty Sweeftiq is (🖋)+(💧), and the vulnerability of the Bloodthirsty Sweeftiq is 🖋💧. Let's make an arena for the combat between the Oolopod and the Bloodthirsty Sweeftiq:

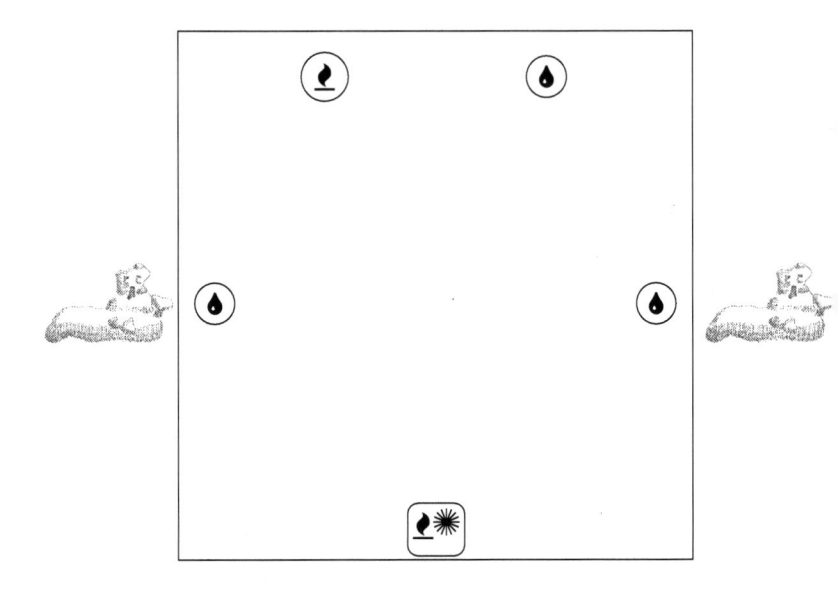

Adding the combat arrows, we get:

4.4. DESIGNER DUELING

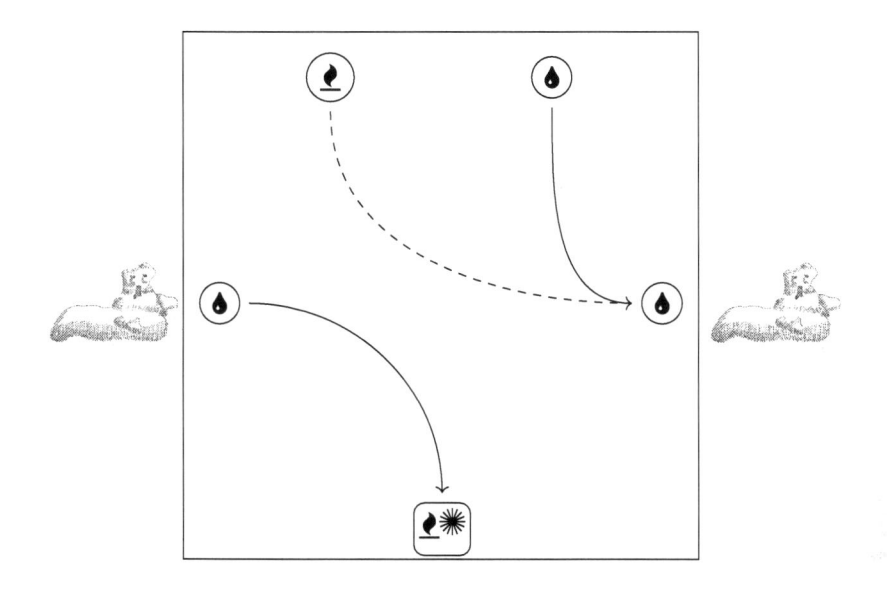

The Oolopod can thus defeat the Bloodthirsty Sweeftiq, and by the tournament rules isn't allowed to be put to the test against the Primeval Gtuftbak

On the other hand, the Bloodthirsty Waynhom we used earlier is still permitted. Let's run a quick combat to show that it *can't* defeat the Bloodthirsty Sweeftiq. We already know both creatures' attacks and vulnerabilities, so we can make the arena:

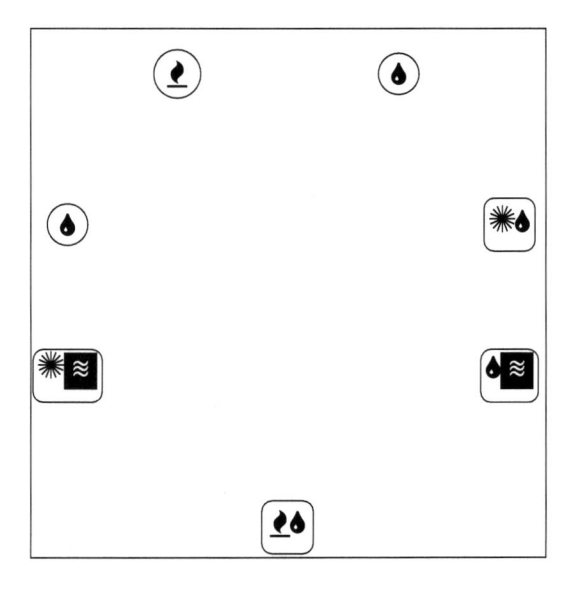

Running the combat, we get:

4.4. DESIGNER DUELING

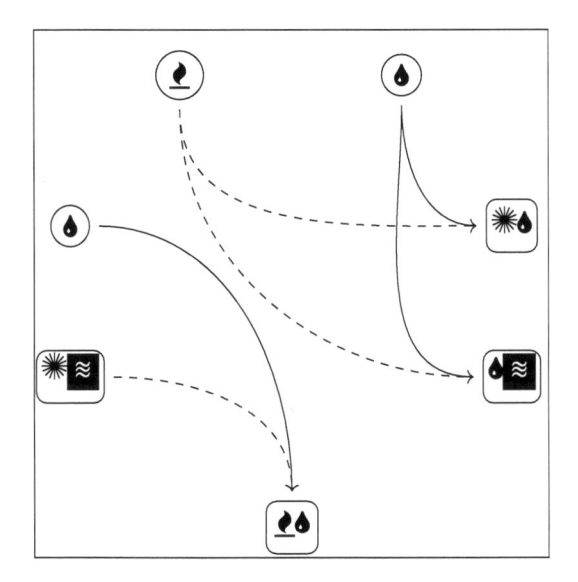

The Bloodthirsty Waynhom is unable to defeat the Bloodthirsty Sweeftiq, because its ⟨※≈⟩ attack component can't exploit the Sweeftiq vulnerability of ⟨👁👁⟩, since there is no overlap between the two. (The Bloodthirsty Sweeftiq can't defeat the Bloodthirsty Waynhom either, but that doesn't matter – we don't actually *want* to fight these two creatures. We just need to see if the Bloodthirsty Waynhom is even allowed into the arena by making sure it isn't so powerful that it can defeat a Bloodthirsty Sweeftiq.)

That means that, having genetically engineered the Bloodthirsty Waynhom from the Schloof and Primeval Quiffex eggs, we are indeed allowed to use it to fight the Primeval Gtuftbak. And we've already seen that in a duel between a Bloodthirsty Waynhom and a Primeval Gtuftbak, the Waynhom emerges victorious. Another win for us!

3. **Multi-Round Duels**: As we've seen, if you're given a Schloof and a Primeval Quiffex egg, you have multiple options for

engineering a creature to defeat a Primeval Gtuftbak in the arena. But now suppose you are given three eggs: the Schloof egg and Primeval Quiffex egg as before, but also an Eldritch Webblob egg. You still have to engineer a creature to defeat a Primeval Gtuftbak, but now you must *also* make a beast to defeat a Bloodthirsty Awtroof. And all of your engineering must be done using only those three eggs.

If you use the Schloof and Primeval Quiffex eggs, as before, to make either an Oolopod or a Bloodthirsty Waynhom to defeat the Primeval Gtuftbak, you'll be left with only the Eldritch Webblob egg to use in preparing to fight the Bloodthirsty Awtroof. And with a little experimenting, you'll discover that there's just nothing you can engineer from an Eldritch Webblob egg that can defeat a Bloodthirsty Awtroof. So you need to use your resources wisely.

Here's one plan that works. First, just hatch the Eldritch Webblob egg and pit the resulting Webblob against the Primeval Gtuftbak. Then use the Schloof and Primeval Quiffex eggs to make an Oolopod (which we've already seen you can do), and have the Oolopod fight the Bloodthirsty Awtroof. Both of these combats will be victories for you.

Let's check and make sure that's right. First, we put the Eldritch Webblob and the Primeval Gtuftbak in the arena. We know all the attacks and vulnerabilities already, so here's the arena:

4.4. DESIGNER DUELING

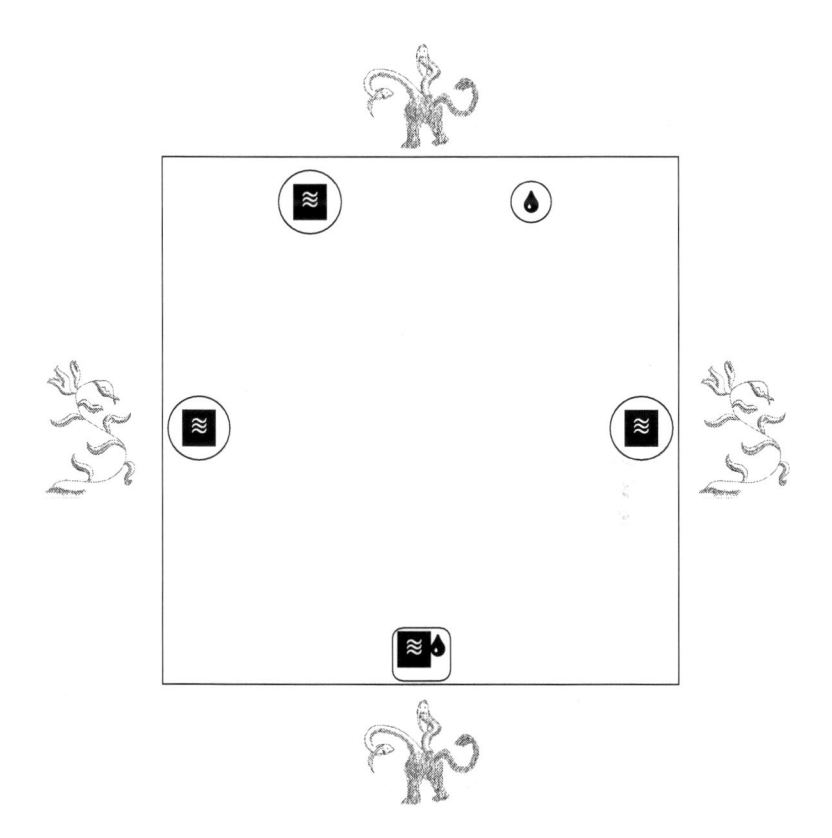

And now the combat:

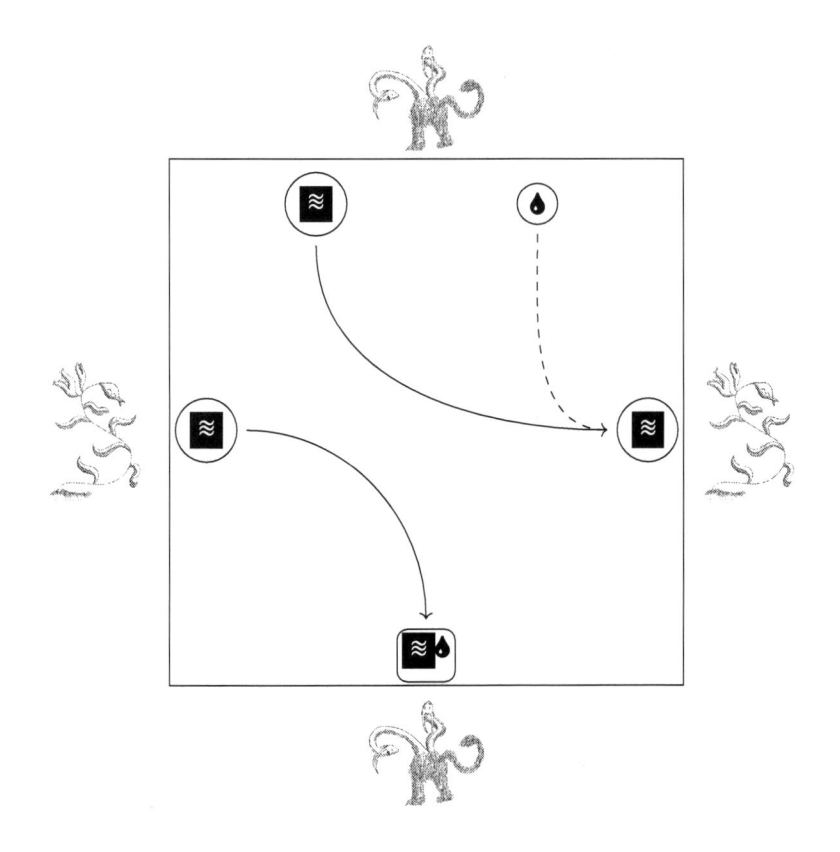

That is, as predicted, a win for the Eldritch Webblob. We also need to check that our Oolopod can defeat the Bloodthirsty Awtroof. We've already seen that a Bloodthirsty Awtroof, having a Fluftoom and an Oolopod as parents, attacks with 💧+💧. Its vulnerability is thus 💧💧. So we can make the arena:

4.4. DESIGNER DUELING

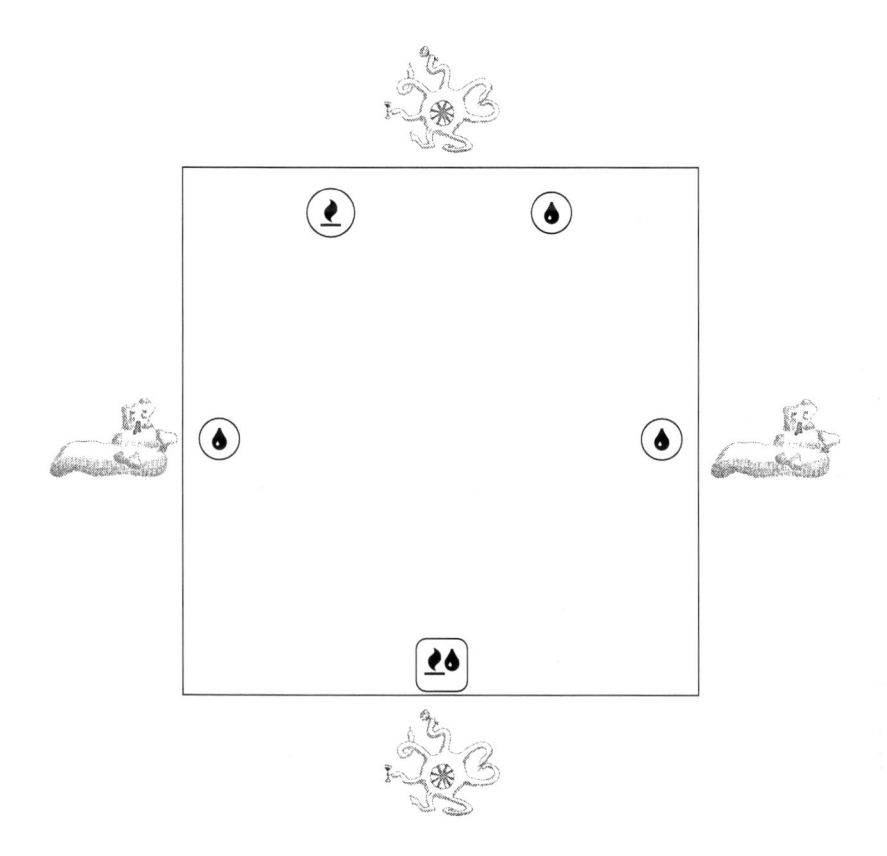

Working out the combat gives us:

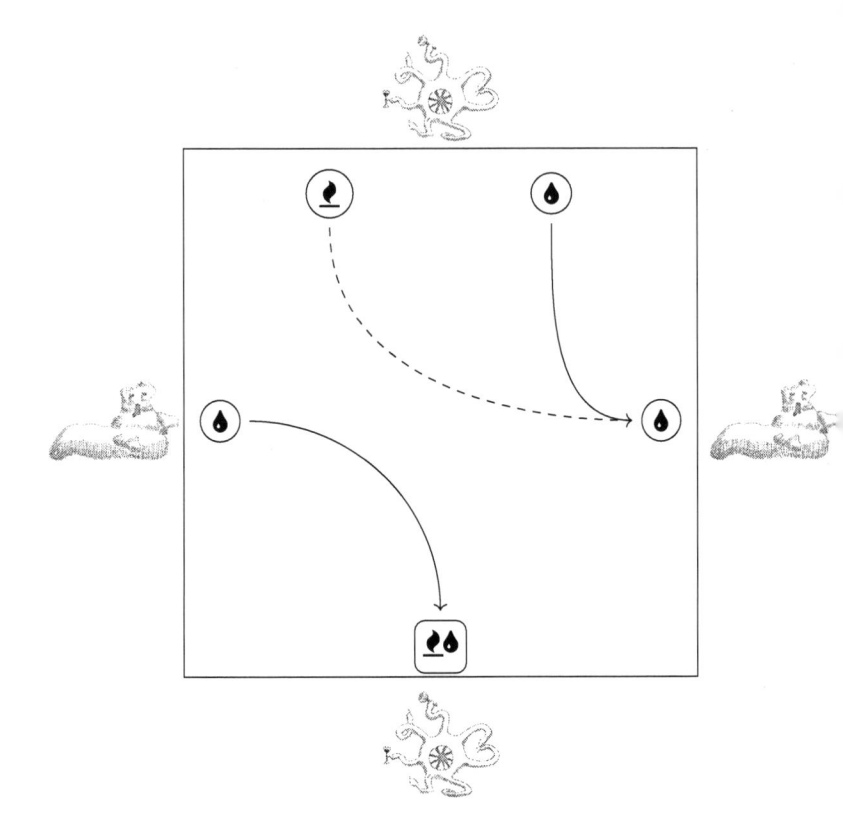

Again as predicted, the Oolopod defeats the Bloodthirsty Awtroof. Multiple round designer duels require especially careful planning, thinking through your starting resources carefully and finding the most efficient genetic routes to sufficiently powerful creatures.

CHAPTER 5
GRAND UNIFIED LOGIBEAST THEORY

The majority of this user's guide, as befits a *user's* guide, has been practical in its aims. Our goal has been to get you up and running as a designing of Logibeasts using your Genetic Manipulator and a dueler of Logibeasts using your Beginner's Arena. For many of you, that will be all you ever wanted, and you're welcome to close this book now and get to work. Some of you, however, may find yourselves intrigued to know more about what's going on under the hood – you may want to *understand*, not just *exploit*, Logibeasts.

Logibeast theory has been a burgeoning area of academic research over the last decade. The work has quickly become far too sophisticated for us to be able to do more than give a very small taste here. If you're excited by what you learn in this chapter, the Amsterdam ILLC program in advanced Logibeast studies is currently the world's leading center in this area, and is currently accepting graduate study applications.

In this chapter, we're going to prove two small results, and then set out a little framework for thinking about the significance of those two results. We'll then use those results as a springboard for stating the core result of Grand Unified Logibeast Theory, but won't attempt to go into any details about that theory. Here are the two results we're going to prove:

First Result: If two Logibeasts have exactly the same

elemental attacks, then a combat between them is always a destructive draw.

Second Result: Any Logibeast has the same elemental attack as its Eldritch grandchild.

So let's get to work proving.

5.1 Proof of the First Result

Our goal is to prove that *any two Logibeasts with the same attacks will fight to a destructive draw*. That's not a claim specifically about, say, the Aarobak and the Eldritch Mumloom, or about the Bloodthirsty Chylziq and the Primeval Achmemth. We need to be thinking more generally about that – not relying on features of any specific beasts. So let's just invent two completely arbitrary beasts to think about. We'll call them the Arbitrary Zizzle and the Arbitrary Zazzle. The Zizzle and the Zazzle could be anything, so if we can prove something about them, we will have proved a general claim about all of the Logibeasts.

We assume that the Arbitrary Zizzle and the Arbitrary Zazzle have the same attacks. Notice that they then also have the same vulnerabilities, since the attack form of a beast fully determines, via the Vulnerability Rule, the vulnerability of that beast. When the Arbitrary Zizzle fights the Arbitrary Zazzle, the result isn't going to be a victory by the Zizzle over the Zazzle. How could it be? Every attack the Zizzle can launch, the Zazzle can launch as well. And every vulnerability the Zazzle has, the Zizzle has as well. A bit more carefully, when the Zizzle fights the Zazzle, the scorekeeping arena looks exactly the same on the horizontal as it does on the vertical – exactly the same attack components, exactly the same vulnerability components. So everywhere there is an arrow from the Zizzle's attacks to the Zazzle's vulnerabilities, there is a corresponding arrow from the Zazzle's attacks to the Zizzle's vulnerabilities. The situation is perfectly symmetric, so whatever happens to the one beast happens to the other. But a victory by the Zizzle over the Zazzle is asymmetric, and thus can't happen.

For the same reason, we aren't going to get a victory by the Zazzle over the Zizzle. That means that there are only two possibilities.

5.1. PROOF OF THE FIRST RESULT

Either the Zizzle and the Zazzle fight to an inconclusive draw, or they fight to a destructive draw. Our goal is to show that it's always a destructive draw. We'll consider two easier special cases, and then look at the result in its full generality.

First Special Case: Say that a creature's attack is *simple* if it is just a single element (or anti-element). So (≈) is a simple attack, as is (♟). But (💧⊕) is not simple, and (💧)+(✹) is not simple. For our first special case, we'll look at the case in which the Zizzle has a simple attack. (Of course, the Zazzle then also has that same simple attack, since we're assuming that Zizzle and Zazzle have the same attack.)

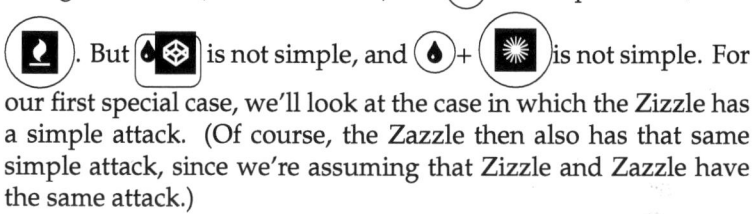

Given the Vulnerability Rule, when a creature has a simple attack, its vulnerability is the same as its attack. Let's use (⏻) as a symbol for some arbitrary simple attack. Then the Zizzle and the Zazzle both have an attack of (⏻) and a vulnerability of (⏻). So here's the arena for a Zizzle versus Zazzle combat:

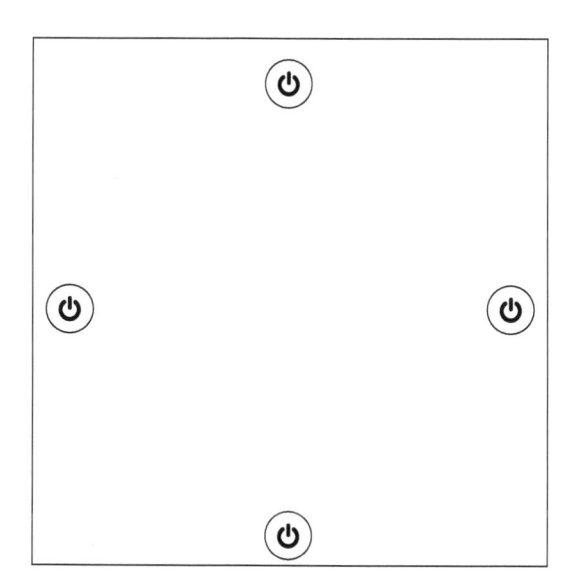

That's an easy combat to resolve:

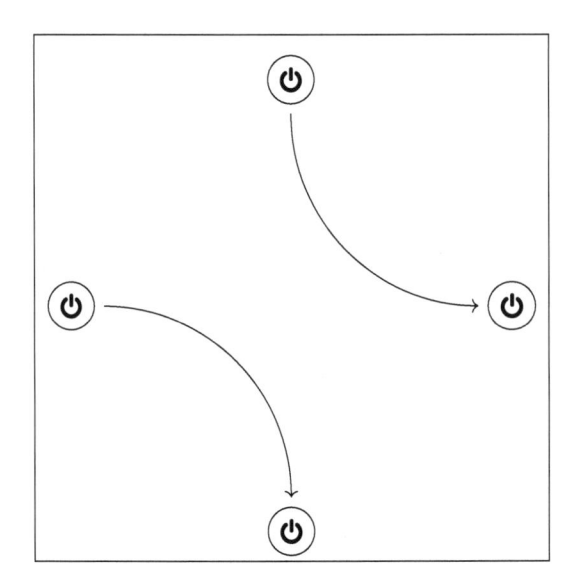

And it's a destructive draw, as predicted.

Second Special Case: Okay, that first case was a bit easy. Let's get slightly more complicated for the next special case. Call an attack *singular* if it's either (a) an attack that's just a stacking of a bunch of elements, with no pulsing, or (b) an attack that's just a pulsing of a bunch of elements, with no stacking. So $\boxed{\approx \blacklozenge \diamondsuit}$ is singular, and $(\blacklozenge) + (\boxed{\text{\normalsize ♟}}) + (\boxed{\text{\normalsize ✹}})$ is singular. But $(\blacklozenge) + \boxed{\approx \text{\normalsize ♟}}$ is not singular.

Assume the Zizzle has a singular attack. (The Zazzle, which has the same attack as the Zizzle, also then has a singular attack.) Let's first look at the case in which the Zizzle's singular attack is a stack of elements. We'll call it $\boxed{\mathbf{\circlearrowleft}_1 \mathbf{\circlearrowleft}_2 \ldots \mathbf{\circlearrowleft}_n}$. Then by the Vulnerability Rule, the vulnerability of the Zizzle is $(\mathbf{\circlearrowleft}_1) + (\mathbf{\circlearrowleft}_2) + \ldots + (\mathbf{\circlearrowleft}_n)$. The Zazzle, of course, has the same attack and the same vulnerability.

Consider what happens when the Zizzle fights the Zazzle. Pick some component of the Zazzle's vulnerability – call it $(\mathbf{\circlearrowleft}_j)$. That

5.1. PROOF OF THE FIRST RESULT

vulnerability component overlaps the Zizzle's attack of $\boxed{⏻_1 ⏻_2 \ldots ⏻_n}$. That's because the Zazzle's vulnerability is just a pulsed sequence of all of the elemental components of the Zizzle's attack, so whatever element features in this component of the Zazzle's vulnerability, it must have been one of the elements in the Zizzle's stacked attack. That means the Zizzle can exploit every vulnerability component of the Zazzle's, so the Zizzle can destroy the Zazzle. But the situation is perfectly symmetric, so for the same reason, the Zazzle can destroy the Zizzle. Once again, it's a destructive draw.

But what if the Zizzle's singular attack is pulsed, rather than stacked? Then its attack looks like $(⏻_1) + (⏻_2) + \ldots + (⏻_n)$. By the Vulnerability Rule, its vulnerability is then $\boxed{⏻_1 ⏻_2 \ldots ⏻_n}$. As before, the Zazzle has the same attack and the same vulnerability as the Zizzle. So let's see what happens when the Zizzle attacks the Zazzle. Since the Zizzle has a pulsed attack, its attack has many components. Pick one of those components, and call it $(⏻_j)$. That attack component overlaps the sole vulnerability component of $\boxed{⏻_1 ⏻_2 \ldots ⏻_n}$, because all of the elements of the pulsed attack are stacked together in the vulnerability. So that attack component can exploit the vulnerability. But $(⏻_j)$ was arbitrary, so what's true of it is true of all of the attack components. Thus each attack component of the Zizzle's can exploit the one vulnerability component of the Zazzle's, and by the All-All Rule the Zizzle can destroy the Zazzle. Again by symmetry, the Zazzle can also destroy the Zizzle, so it's a destructive draw.

With the two special cases out of the way, let's consider the Zizzle versus Zazzle battle in more generality. The Zizzle's attack can now be anything. So in general we can think of it as a pulsed sequence of a bunch of stacked attacks, with each stack combining a bunch of elements. We can think of the whole thing as forming a kind of rectangle:

$$\begin{array}{cccc} \text{⏻}_{1,1} & \text{⏻}_{1,2} & \cdots & \text{⏻}_{1,n} \\ \text{⏻}_{2,1} & \text{⏻}_{2,2} & \cdots & \text{⏻}_{2,n} \\ \cdots & \cdots & \cdots & \cdots \\ \text{⏻}_{m,1} & \text{⏻}_{m,2} & \cdots & \text{⏻}_{m,n} \end{array}$$

(That picture isn't perfectly general, because it shows m pulsed attack components each of which has the same number n of stacked elements, and in fact different pulsed components could contain different numbers of stacked elements. But it's good enough to give the general idea.) Now, what happens when we apply the Vulnerability Rule to that attack to create the Zizzle's vulnerability? We get a huge pulsed vulnerability in which each stacked component picks one item from each row of the rectangle. The components of the vulnerability are, in essence, *vertical paths through the rectangle*. (Not necessarily straight-line paths.)

As before, the Zazzle has the same attack and vulnerability as the Zizzle. We now claim that each component of the Zizzle's pulsed attack can exploit each component of the Zazzle's vulnerability. Pick some component of the Zizzle's attack. That's the same as picking some row of the rectangle. Call that the *selected row*. Now pick some component of the Zazzle's vulnerability. That's the same as some vertical path through the rectangle. But that vertical path has to pick *something* from the selected row. Whatever that something is, it will be a point of overlap between the attack component and the vulnerability component. Thus the attack component exploits the vulnerability component. The reasoning was completely general though – it works for any attack component and any vulnerability component. Thus every attack component of the Zizzle exploits every vulnerability component of the Zazzle, ad by the All-All Rule the Zizzle can destroy the Zazzle.

As usual, the situation is fully symmetric, so the Zazzle can also destroy the Zizzle. Thus it's a destructive draw. That gives us the First Result. Whenever two Logibeasts of the same attack fight, the result is a Destructive Draw.

5.2 Proof of the Second Result

Our goal is to prove that any beast has the same attack as its Eldritch grandparent. As with the first result, let's consider a couple of special cases before considering the result in its full general-

5.2. PROOF OF THE SECOND RESULT

ity. We'll continue to talk about our arbitrary beast the Aribirary Zizzle, and let the Eldritch Zozzle be our name for the Eldritch child of the Zizzle, and the Eldritch Eldritch Zuzzle be the Eldritch *grandchild* of the Zizzle (and hence the Eldritch child of the Zozzle).

First Special Case: First assume the Zizzle has a simple attack. Call it ⏻. Then the Eldritch Zozzle attacks with the anti-element of ⏻, or ⏻. And then the Eldritch Eldritch Zuzzle attacks with the anti-element of ⏻, which is ⏻. We're right back where we started, so the Zizzle and its Eldritch grandparent the Zuzzle have the same attack.

Second Special Case: That was almost too easy. Let's make it a little harder by assuming the Zizzle has a singular attack. If the Zizzle's singular attack is a stacked attack $\boxed{⏻_1 ⏻_2 \ldots ⏻_n}$, then by the Eldritch Rule, the Eldritch Zozzle's attack will convert the stack into a pulse and each element into its anti-element, giving us $(⏻_1) + (⏻_2) + \ldots + (⏻_n)$. And then the Eldritch Eldritch Zuzzle's attack will apply the Eldritch Rule to that pulsed attack. That converts the pulsed attack into a stacked attack, and converts each element into its anti-element, bringing the elements back to their starting point. That gives us our starting $\boxed{⏻_1 ⏻_2 \ldots ⏻_n}$. The Eldritch Eldritch Zuzzle does indeed have the same attack as the Aribtrary Zizzle.

Now we can tackle the fully general case. Things get a bit messy here. As in the First Result, the fully general case is a Zizzle with an attack that is a pulsed sequence of stacked attacks, which we can represent using the rectangle:

$$\begin{array}{|cccc|} \hline ⏻_{1,1} & ⏻_{1,2} & \ldots & ⏻_{1,n} \\ ⏻_{2,1} & ⏻_{2,2} & \ldots & ⏻_{2,n} \\ \ldots & \ldots & \ldots & \ldots \\ ⏻_{m,1} & ⏻_{m,2} & \ldots & ⏻_{m,n} \\ \hline \end{array}$$

We apply the Eldritch Rule to this to get the attack of the Eldritch

Zozzle. All of the elements turn into their anti-elements. Each row of the rectangle is a stacked attack component, so it gets converted into a pulsed component. And then we stack together all of those pulses. As before, that's a matter of taking vertical paths through the rectangle. So the attack of the Eldritch Zozzle is a long pulsed sequence of inverted vertical paths through the rectangle. (Inverted because the elemental components of the vertical paths have all been changed into their anti-elements.)

And now we need to apply the Eldritch Rule to *that*, to get the attack of the Eldritch Eldritch Zuzzle. Once again, elements get replaced by their anti-elements. That's good – each $\left(\overline{\mathbf{\Phi}_{j,k}}\right)$ has been converted to $\left(\mathbf{\Phi}_{j,k}\right)$ and then back to $\left(\mathbf{\Phi}_{j,k}\right)$ again, so we're back with the same elements that made up the attack of the Zizzle. But we also need to convert the stacked components of the Eldritch Zozzle's attacks to pulses, the pulsed components of the Zozzle's attacks to stacks, and apply the Box Method.

The stacks of the Zozzle's attack are the individual vertical paths through the Zizzle's rectangle. So each vertical path gets made into a pulse. We then stack *all* of the possible vertical paths. When we apply the Box Method to that, we get stacks that pick one element from each vertical path. All of those stacks then get pulsed.

That's a lot to take in. Let's look at a small example. Suppose the Zizzle has a rectangle like this:

| A | B | C |
| D | E | F |

(We'll just use letters in place of specific elements, since we don't care what the elements are for this example.) That means that the Zizzle has the attack ABC + DEF. It pulses a stack of element A, B, and C with a stack of elements D, E, and F. Then the Eldritch Zozzle has an attack of $\overline{AD} + \overline{AE} + \overline{AF} + \overline{BD} + \overline{BE} + \overline{BF} + \overline{CD} + \overline{CE} + \overline{CF}$. (The overlining here represents the anti-element of each off the original elements.) The nine pulsed components correspond to the nine vertical paths through the rectangle.

5.2. PROOF OF THE SECOND RESULT

To get the attack of the Eldritch Eldritch Zuzzle, we then make a rectangle for the Eldritch Zozzle's attack, which looks like this:

$\overline{A}$	$\overline{D}$
$\overline{A}$	$\overline{E}$
$\overline{A}$	$\overline{F}$
$\overline{B}$	$\overline{D}$
$\overline{B}$	$\overline{E}$
$\overline{B}$	$\overline{F}$
$\overline{C}$	$\overline{D}$
$\overline{C}$	$\overline{E}$
$\overline{C}$	$\overline{F}$

We take the anti-element of each element in this rectangle, which just gets rid of the overlining and sends everything back to the original A, B, C, D, E, and F. And then we take all vertical paths through the rectangle, and pulse them together.

But there are a *lot* of vertical paths through the rectangle. On each row we have two choices, and there are nine rows, so there are $2^9 = 512$ paths. The Eldritch Eldritch Zuzzle is going to have an attack with 512 pulsed components, then. That's quite a pain to write out, and definitely not the same as the attack of the starting Zizzle.

Fortunately, there's a lot of repetition in those 512 components. Consider the path that takes the left A from the first row, and then the right entry from each row after that (the path LRRRRRRRR). That path produces the stacked component AEFDEFDEF. By Simplification, that's the same as ADEF. But the path LLRRRRRRR produces the staked component AAFDEFDEF, which also simplifies to ADEF. So we don't need to include both of those pulses – they amount to the same thing.

Doing all the simplifying we can, we get down to 15 remaining non-redundant pulsed components. They are, for the record, ABC, ABCD, ABCE, ABCF, ABCDE, ABCDF, ABCEF, ABCDEF, ADEF, BDEF, CDEF, ABDEF, ACDEF, and BCDEF. That's still a lot to deal with. But there's an interesting pattern to be seen in what remain. *Each pulse either contains all of A, B, and C, or all of D, E, and F.* Let's see why that's true.

Consider the vertical paths through the Eldritch Zozzle's height-9 attack rectangle. Suppose we *don't* pick A from any of the first three rows. Then we *do* pick all of D, E, and F during those three rows. The first three rows are our only chance to pick A, so if we don't pick A, we do pick all of D, E, and F.

For the same reason, if we don't pick B, we do pick all of D, E, and F. And if we don't pick C, we do pick all of D, E, and F. So if we don't pick all of A, B, and C, we fail to pick at least one of them, which means we do pick all of D, E, and F.

So the Eldritch Eldritch Zuzzle's attack consists of pulsed components each of which has either the form ABCetc. or DEFetc. That's an improvement, but it's still not the same as the Zizzle's attack, which was just ABC + DEF. To finish things off, we need to introduce a more advanced form of Simplification:

> **Advanced Rule of Simplification**: If an attack has two pulsed components, and one component is a *subset* of the other, with every element in the smaller component also appearing in the larger component, then the *larger* component can be removed.

Advanced Simplification, for example, tells us that $\boxed{\approx\blacklozenge} + \boxed{\approx\!\!\blacklozenge\!\blacklozenge}$ simplifies to $\boxed{\approx\blacklozenge}$. We didn't bother with Advanced Simplification before, because your work-a-day duelist can get by fine without thinking about such complications. But for the theorist, it's a very helpful tool.

(Why does Advanced Simplification make sense? Well, suppose an attack has a Small Component and a Big Component, and Advanced Simplification is telling us we can get rid of the Big Component. Any vulnerability component exploited by the Small Component is also going to be exploited by the Big Component – if there's overlap with Small, there will also be overlap with Big. So when the All-All Rule is met with just the Small Component, it is also met with the Big Component. And when the All-All Rule isn't met by the Small Component, we've already failed to defeat the opponent, and it won't matter whether the Big Component is included or not.)

Using Advanced Simplification, the Eldritch Eldritch Zuzzle's attack simplifies to ABC + DEF, which is the same as the Zizzle's, as desired.

OK, we've got the basic idea now, but we're still not quite there, because we've been considering the special case in which the Zizzle has the attack ABC + DEF. Let's return to the general case in which the Zizzle's attack is some:

⏻$_{1,1}$	⏻$_{1,2}$	...	⏻$_{1,n}$
⏻$_{2,1}$	⏻$_{2,2}$	...	⏻$_{2,n}$
...	...	...	...
⏻$_{m,1}$	⏻$_{m,2}$	...	⏻$_{m,n}$

The same idea applies; it's just a bit messier. The Eldritch Zozzle's attack is the pulsing of the stacking of all the vertical paths through this rectangle (with the elements inverted). And the Eldritch Eldritch Zuzzle's attack is then the pulsing of the stacking of all the vertical paths through the *Zozzle's* rectangle. But then, as before, each stack in the Zuzzle's attack contains all the elements in some row of the Zizzle's original rectangle. That's because for each element in a given row, if that element isn't contained at all, the vertical path has to instead select entirely from the other side of the Zozzle's rectangle. (That's a bit hand-wavy. A more careful proof requires mathematical induction.)

So once again the Zuzzle's attack consists of a lot of pulses each of which contains as a subset a row of the Zizzle's rectangle. (That is, one of the stacked components of the Zizzle's pulsed attack.) By Advanced Simplification, the Eldritch Eldritch Zuzzle's attack is then the same as that of the Zizzle. That gives us what we need to establish the Second Result.

5.3 A Brief Glance at Grand Unified Logibeast Theory

We've now seen a general fact about attacks and duels: any two creatures with exactly the same attacks have a destructive draw when they fight. And we've seen a specific fact about genealogy and attacks: the Eldritch grandchild of a creature has the same attack as the original creature. Putting these two facts together, we immediately learn that any creature will have a destructive draw with its Eldritch grandchild.

That fact is suggestive when we remember that from any creature we can genetically engineer its Eldritch grandchild, and from any Eldritch grandchild we can genetically engineer its grandparent. A quick reminder of the recipes for these bits of engineering:

Eggs	Step	Genetic Method	Input Creatures	Output Creature
(Eldritch Eldritch Zuzzle)	1	Hatch	-	Eldritch Eldritch Zuzzle
(Eldritch Eldritch Zuzzle)	2	Eldritch Split	1	Zizzle

And:

Eggs	Step	Genetic Method	Input Creatures	Output Creature
(Zizzle)	1	Hatch	-	Zizzle
(Eldritch Zozzle)	2	Hatch	-	Eldritch Zozzle
(Zizzle)	3	Eldritch Merge	1,2,1	Eldritch Eldritch Zuzzle

So from a Zizzle we can engineer an Eldritch Eldritch Zuzzle, and from an Eldritch Eldritch Zuzzle we can engineer a Zizzle. And the Zizzle and Eldritch Eldritch Zuzzle then fight to a destructive draw. That suggests a hypothesis:

> **Hypothesis**: If a Zizzle and a Zazzle can be engineered each from the other, then they fight to a destructive draw.

That hypothesis is true. But it's actually still a specific instance of an even more general result.

The more general result is the crowning result of Logibeast theory: the central theorem of Grand Unified Logibeast Theory:

> **Central Theorem**: An Arbitrary Zizzle can destroy an Arbitrary Zazzle in combat if and only if the Zazzle can be engineered from the Zizzle.

The Central Theorem, being an "if and only if" claim, tells us two things. First, it tells us that when you engineer a Zazzle from a Zizzle, you're going to get a creature that the Zizzle can destroy. (That doesn't mean the Zizzle will be *victorious* in combat. The Zazzle might also be able to destroy the Zizzle, in which case it will be a destructive draw. But it can't be an inconclusive draw or a victory for the Zazzle.) And second, if your Zizzle can destroy a Zazzle in combat, then there's some way to engineer a Zazzle from

5.3. A BRIEF GLANCE AT GRAND UNIFIED LOGIBEAST THEORY

a Zizzle. The Central Theorem provides a deep and foundational link between the genetic structure of Logibeasts and their combat abilities.

Here ends our little guided tour of Logibeast theory. We aren't going to prove the Central Theorem, or even begin to explore the many fascinating consequences of that theorem – even a hand-waving trip through that further territory requires more time and energy than we're willing to ask of you here. (*The Metametamathematics of Metalogibeasts* and *Logibeasts and Logicomputability* are two excellent treatments of these topics, if both rather formidable to the novice.) We hope, however, we've shown you enough to induce you to book a further tour of your own, and we wish you the best of travels through the exciting land of Logibeast theory.

CHAPTER 6

THE LOGIBESTIARY

1. **Basic Logibeasts:**

    (a) Fluftoom [ ]

    (b) Yttrig [ ]

    (c) Aarobak [ ]

    (d) Schloof [ ]

    (e) Oolopod [ ]

2. **Grotesque Logibeasts:**

    (a) Ooolopd + Ytrrig ⇒ Grotesque Ogrit [ ]

CHAPTER 6. THE LOGIBESTIARY

(b) Oolopod + Fluftoom ⇒ Grotesque Gnuffle [   ]

(c) Yttrig + Eldritch Webblob ⇒ Grotesque Ffli [   ]
(d) Grotesque Ogrit + Eldritch Whylxot ⇒ Grotesque Uuhulmo [   ]

(e) Eldritch Whylxot + Oolopod ⇒ Grotesque Hjunkit [   ]
(f) Primeval Gtuftbak + Primeval J'jaklu ⇒ Grotesque Qeqesflon [   ]
(g) Grotesque Gnuffle + Grotesque Ffli ⇒ Grotesque Ushtrimbot [   ]
(h) Bloodthirsty Awtroof + Bloodthirsty Cavaidko ⇒ Grotesque Oivuut [   ]
(i) Bloodthirsty Blijjif + Bloodthirsty Azill ⇒ Grotesque Tvunglit []
(j) Eldritch Webblob + Yttrig ⇒ Grotesque Yazzil []

3. **Primeval Logibeasts**:

(a) Fluftoom + Aarobak ⇒ Primeval Schniftoo []

(b) Schloof + Yttrig ⇒ Primeval Knug [   ]

(c) Oolopod + Fluftoom ⇒ Primeval Dessifto [   ]

(d) Oolopod + Oolopod ⇒ Primeval Protopod [   ]

(e) Schloof + Grotesque Ogrit ⇒ Primeval Quiffex [   ]

(f) Aarobak + Oolopod ⇒ Primeval Gtuftbak [   ]
(g) Oolopod + Aarobak ⇒ Primeval J'jaklu []
(h) Bloodthirsty Awtroof + Aarobak ⇒ Primeval Vringxed []
(i) Yttrig + Primeval J'jaklu ⇒ Primeval Gnomoloq []
(j) Grotesque Ffli + Eldritch Iumhfiss ⇒ Primeval Vrilvriktu []
(k) Primeval Gnomoloq + Primeval Vrilvriktu ⇒ Primeval Achmemth []
(l) Primeval J'jaklu + Aarobak ⇒ Primeval Inxam []

4. **Winged Logibeasts:**

(a) Aarobak + Oolopod ⇒ Winged Hvornid [   ]

(b) Oolopod + Fluftoom ⇒ Winged Xeerun [   ]

(c) Yttrig + Grotesque Ogrit ⇒ Winged Shugraat [   ]
(d) Eldritch M'bimtip + Grotesque Ogrit ⇒ Winged Caicarx []

5. **Bloodthirsty Logibeasts:**

172   CHAPTER 6. THE LOGIBESTIARY

(a) Oolopod + Fluftoom ⇒ Bloodthirsty Awtroof [   ]

(b) Schloof + Oolopod ⇒ Bloodthirsty Cavaidko [   ]
(c) Fluftoom + Eldritch Foorghast ⇒ Bloodthirsty Chylziq
[   ]

(d) Schloof + Grotesque Gnuffle ⇒ Bloodthirsty Azill [   ]
(e) Bloodthirsty Awtroof + Bloodthirsty Cavaidko ⇒ Bloodthirsty Blijjif [   ]
(f) Oolopod + Grotesque Yazzil ⇒ Bloodthirsty Waynhom []
(g) Oolopod + Fluftoom ⇒ Bloodthirsty Sweeftiq []

6. **Eldritch Beasts**:

(a) Aarobak ⇒ Eldritch Webblob [   ]

(b) Oolopod ⇒ Eldritch Iumhfiss [   ]

(c) Yttrig ⇒ Eldritch M'bimtip [   ]
(d) Schloof ⇒ Eldritch Izghaam []
(e) Eldritch Webblob ⇒ Eldritch Mumfloom []

(f) Fluftoom ⇒ Eldritch Foorghast []
(g) Bloodthirsty Chylziq ⇒ Eldritch Whyndidid []
(h) Eldritch Whyndidid ⇒ Eldritch Rhozoon []
(i) Primeval J'jaklu ⇒ Eldritch Effintop []
(j) Eldritch Iumhfiss ⇒ Eldritch Iamimtu []
(k) Grotesque Ffli ⇒ Eldritch F'nafkor []
(l) Grotesque Oivutt ⇒ Eldritch Dkbaino []
(m) Primeval Achmemth ⇒ Eldritch Whylxot []

Made in the USA
Lexington, KY
20 August 2018